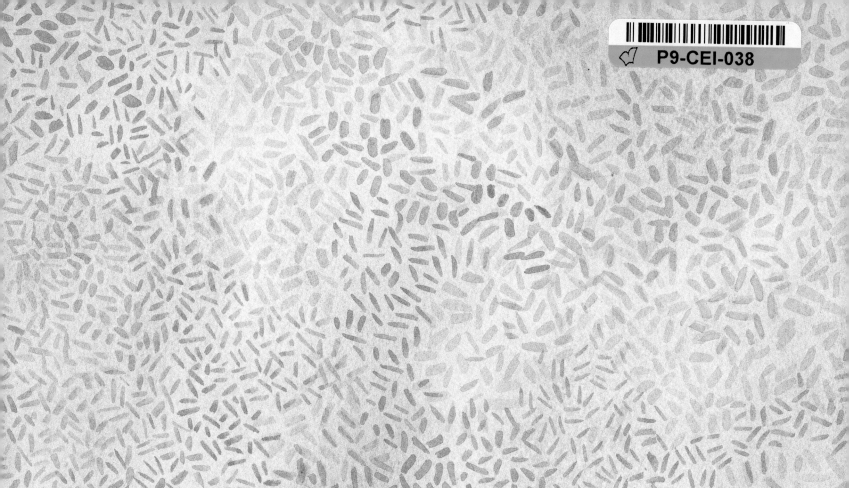

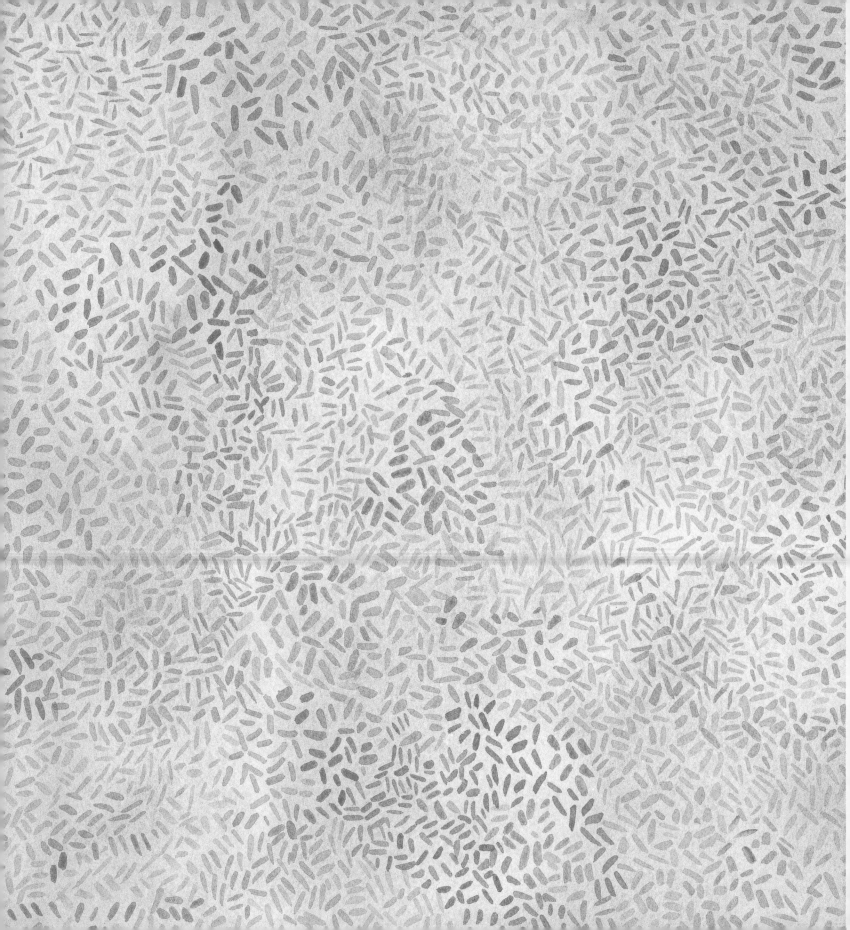

Better Homes and Gardens®

crafts
TO MAKE & SELL

Better Homes and Gardens® Books
Des Moines, Iowa

Better Homes and Gardens® Books
An imprint of Meredith® Books

Crafts to Make & Sell
Editor: Carol Field Dahlstrom
Technical Editor: Susan M. Banker
Graphic Designer: Angela Haupert Hoogensen
Copy Chief: Catherine Hamrick
Copy and Production Editor: Terri Fredrickson
Contributing Copy Editor: Carol Boker
Contributing Proofreaders: Diane Doro, Kathy Eastman,
    Colleen Johnson
Technical Illustrator: Chris Neubauer Graphics, Inc.
Electronic Production Coordinator: Paula Forest
Editorial and Design Assistants: Judy Bailey, Mary Lee Gavin,
    Karen Schirm
Production Director: Douglas M. Johnston
Book Production Managers: Pam Kvitne, Marjorie J. Schenkelberg

Meredith® Books
Editor in Chief: James D. Blume
Design Director: Matt Strelecki
Managing Editor: Gregory H. Kayko

Director, Sales & Marketing, Retail: Michael A. Peterson
Director, Sales & Marketing, Special Markets: Rita McMullen
Director, Sales & Marketing, Home & Garden Center Channel:
    Ray Wolf
Director, Operations: George A. Susral

Vice President, General Manager: Jamie L. Martin

Better Homes and Gardens® Magazine
Editor in Chief: Jean LemMon

Meredith Publishing Group
President, Publishing Group: Christopher M. Little
Vice President, Consumer Marketing & Development:
    Hal Oringer

Meredith Corporation
Chairman and Chief Executive Officer: William T. Kerr

Chairman of the Executive Committee: E. T. Meredith III

All of us at Better Homes and Gardens® Books are dedicated
to providing you with information and ideas to create wonderful
crafts projects. We welcome your comments and suggestions.
Write to us at: Better Homes and Gardens Books,
Crafts Editorial Department, 1716 Locust St., Des Moines, IA
50309-3023.

If you would like to purchase any of our books, check wherever
quality books are sold. Visit our website at bhg.com or
bhgbooks.com.

Cover Photograph: Peter Krumhardt
Watercolor Illustration: Alice Wetzel

LET THE CRAFTING BEGIN!

If you are a die-hard crafter who enjoys selling your handmade projects (or has dreamed of it), then get ready to be inspired as never before.

This book is truly a one-of-a-kind reference book for crafters. Whether you display at craft shows across the country or simply enjoy sharing your talents as gifts for friends and family, this project-packed book will give you step-by-step instructions and suggestions for creating your own works of art.

Enjoy hundreds of tips on where to find supplies, how to display your crafts at a show, variations to make each project unique (or more time- or cost-effective), and suggestions for pricing each item. You'll also find secret crafting tips—directly from the pros—so that each project is successful and has the professional polish you strive for when creating your crafts. For quick reference, there are symbols (shown at *right*) to help guide you in making your crafting decisions.

No matter what techniques you've already tried, this informative and creative book will help you master the types of crafts that are so

 SOURCES—tips on where to find various crafting supplies

 CRAFTING TIPS—expert tips to help along the way

 COSTS AND PRICING—costs involved and suggested selling prices

 TIMESAVING TIPS—ways to make the most of your crafting time

 SELLING SUGGESTIONS—display ideas to bring in sales

 GIFT-GIVING IDEAS—clever ways to present your crafts as gifts

popular at shows today. So get ready to have the crafting time of your life, and don't be surprised if you make quite a profit to boot!

Carol Field Dahlstrom

TABLE OF CONTENTS

PAINT IT!

Whether you enjoy painting on glass, wood, or fabric, this project-packed chapter will inspire you to spend many fun (and profitable) hours with your paints and brushes.

WITH NEEDLE AND THREAD

If you love to sew, get ready to create clever home organizers, extra-special hot pads, terrific mittens, pillows of all kinds, and a whole lot more!

MAKE IT WITH WOOD

A saw cut here, a little sanding there, and you'll soon be making woodcrafts to sell with pride! No experience needed—we'll guide you every step of the way.

IT'S ALWAYS CHRISTMAS

Celebrate the season of all seasons with crafts that are as wondrous as the holiday itself.
Paint, sew, etch—the choice is yours!

FLORAL AND NATURE

Get a little closer to nature by creating works of art using the bounty around you.
Purchase the nature supplies or gather them outdoors to make your crafting treasures.

FLEA MARKET TRANSFORMATIONS

You (or your customers) won't be able to resist these fun-to-make projects. You'll soon
shop flea markets and garage sales with a whole new outlook.

PAINT
IT!

Never out of style and always in demand,

painted accessories are highlighted in this bright chapter.

From wintry mugs to crackled frames,

itsy-bitsy pushpins to glowing lamps and shades,

these projects will make you eager to spend time

with your paints and brushes.

WITH BRUSH IN HAND

Enhancing Objects with Paint

With all of the paints available today, you can embellish nearly anything. Whether you are working on metal, wood, glass, plastic, fabric, or any other surface, chances are you can find a paint that is specifically made for that medium. And don't limit yourself to supplies found in craft stores—be sure to check out what's available in automotive shops, home centers, hardware stores, and discount stores.

Depending on the type of paint chosen and the technique used, painted projects can take on several different looks. To achieve a country, primitive, or antique feel, you may want to sand a project after painting. A crackling medium or an antiquing stain can also lend a vintage flair to your work. For a more contemporary finish, enamel or metallic paints may be a wise choice. A good way to select paints to add to your crafting supplies is to experiment and decide which types and brands work best for your crafting needs.

Selling Painted Items

Before selecting the types of projects you want to paint and sell, first decide where you want to sell them. For some crafts shows, it may be best to choose very simple projects that take little time and money to make. For more sophisticated art exhibits, you can usually make your pieces distinctive and therefore can charge more per item.

A small touch that adds value is placing the artist's signature and date on a painted item. However, don't let your signature overpower your design, include it simply as a symbol of originality.

To encourage multiple sales, paint items using various color palettes. Then group items in the same tones so customers can visualize how the different pieces you are selling coordinate with one another.

To protect your painted works of art while in transit, be sure to pack them carefully. Bubble wrap works well. Newspapers can be used for some items, as long as items are wrapped in white paper first. This is a must as newsprint can rub off and ruin a project.

If your project has special care instructions, make copies of the instructions and give one with each purchase. If the instructions are short, print them on the back of your business card—it's great customer service and good advertising!

When setting up for a show, be sure to use extra wrapping material so customers feel confident their purchased items will remain in perfect condition while they continue shopping.

frosty mug

This happy fellow won't ever melt when created with permanent glass paints. "Dress" each snowman in the same wintertime attire, or give each one with its own clothing. The quick-to-paint snowflakes are made with a pencil eraser dipped in paint, while the buttons and face details that bring this snowman to life are made with the handle end of a paintbrush.

Sources
- Purchase mugs of all sizes and shapes in discount stores, home decor stores, thrift shops, and crafts stores.
- A variety of glass paints are available in arts and crafts stores.

Painting tips
- To make dots, use a dowel if you don't have a round-tip pencil eraser available.
- Place hand in mug to steady it while painting.

Cost to make project
Approximately $3

Suggested selling price
$9 for one, $17 for two

Time to make project
20 minutes

Timesaving tips
- Paint 6 to 10 mugs at once.
- Paint all the snowmen first, then the snow, etc. This assembly-line process will speed up production.

What you need
Glass mug
Foam plate
High-gloss acrylic enamel glass paints, such as Liquitex Glossies, in white, purple, aqua, blue, pink, magenta, black, and orange
Paintbrushes
Pencil with round-tip eraser

What to do
1. When choosing a mug, look for one that is either glass or a ceramic with a high-gloss glaze. The mug must also be able to withstand a low temperature in the oven if painted with a glass paint that needs to be baked for permanency (read the manufacturer's label on your glass paint).
2. Wash the mug thoroughly and let it air-dry. Do not dry with a cloth as it may leave flecks of dust that will show up in the paint. Avoid touching the surfaces to be painted.

continued on page 12

TO SELL IT
- Display some of the mugs using the gift-giving ideas, *below,* and in a place setting.
- Wrap the mugs individually in tissue first, then in newspapers (so the print does not rub off on the painted surface).
- Offer a discount when a pair is purchased.
- Use a variety of mug colors.
- On the back of a business card, write the care instructions such as, the paints are permanent, wash gently by hand, and do not use in the microwave.
- Display a sign that shouts the savings when purchasing a pair.
- Display mugs at different heights for visibility.

TO GIVE IT
- Fill the mug with cocoa or cider mix, candy canes, or coffee beans.
- Wrap the mug in cellophane and tie at top with ribbon.
- Give a set of mugs in a basket, cushioning them with a wintertime kitchen towel, linen napkins, or a plaid scarf.

frosty mug

▼ **3.** Put a small amount of each color of paint onto a foam plate. To paint the snowman's body, load a small flat paintbrush with white paint and dip a corner of the brush in purple. Paint a couple of strokes on the foam plate to blend the colors.

▶ **4.** Paint three circles on the mug front, leaving about 1 inch above and below (do not apply paint near the rim of the mug).

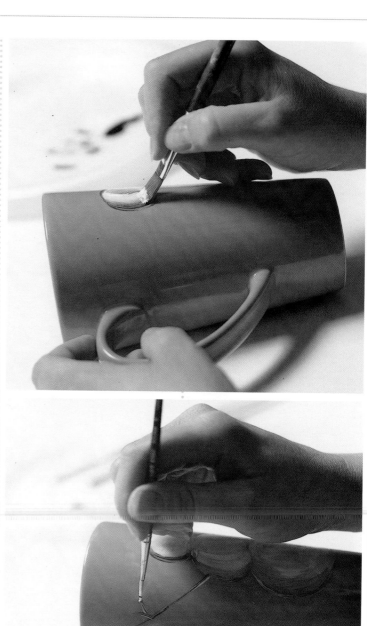

▶ **5.** Use a blend of black and white paints and a fine liner pantbrush to add stick arms.

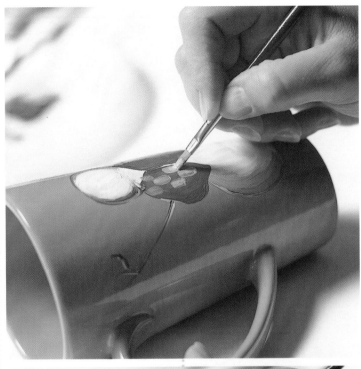

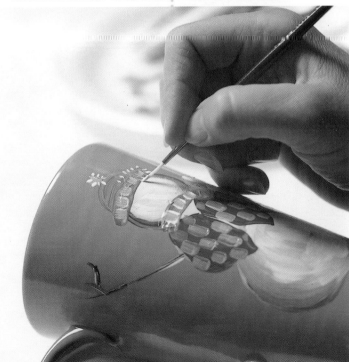

◀ **6.** Paint a purple vest on the snowman as shown, following the shape of the center circle. To add a check design, use a ¼-inch flat paintbrush and pink and magenta.

9. Paint the snow at the base of the mug in the same manner as the snowman body, using white blended with small amounts of aqua, blue, and purple.

◀ **7.** Add a magenta scarf and hat using the same flat brush. Add pink stripes as desired. Use a small pointed paintbrush to add white trim to the hatband and pom-pom edges.

▲ **8.** While the snowman shape is drying, paint the falling snow. Dip the pencil eraser in white paint and carefully dab it on the mug surface, being sure to avoid the rim area.

10. To add eyes and mouth, dip the end of a paintbrush into black paint and dot on the snowman. Add magenta buttons in the same manner. Add a carrot nose using orange paint. Let the paint dry thoroughly.
11. To make the paint permanent, you may need to bake the mug in the oven. Read the paint manufacturer's instructions for proper care of your painted pieces.

whimsical bowls

Serve up a helping of pure fun! These colorfully painted wood bowls hold anything from wrapped treats to small office supplies. Paint the designs shown, or create your own quick and clever motifs for the inside and outside of the bowls.

What you need

Newspapers; wood salad bowls
White spray primer
Small can or disposable cup
Acrylic paints in lime green, grass green, yellow, pink, purple, aqua, royal blue, lavender, pumpkin, and dark red
Fine liner, medium flat, and small round paintbrushes
Pencil with round-tip eraser
Tracing or typing paper
Scissors
Spray acrylic gloss varnish

What to do

1. In a well-ventilated area, cover work surface with newspapers. Place bowls on newspaper. Spray primer on bowls until lightly covered. Let dry. Spray a second coat. Let dry. Turn bowls over and rest on a small can or disposable cup so the rims do not touch the newspaper. Spray two coats on bowl bottoms, allowing to dry between coats.
2. Paint the bowls solid on the inside. Let dry. Turn over and paint the outside and bottoms. Let dry. Apply second coats. Let dry.
3. Refer to the patterns and colors used in the photos, *pages 14 and 16,* or choose your own. Draw shapes on bowls using pencil. For the large flower design, trace pattern and cut out. Trace around pattern in the center of bowl. Paint triangles, flowers, leaves, or any design. Let dry. Outline the shapes with a fine liner brush. Paint smooth, wavy, or straight lines with a fine liner brush. Add dots by dipping the handle end of a paintbrush or round pencil eraser in paint and carefully dotting onto the surface. Layer small dots on top of big dots, if desired. Let dry.
4. Spray the bowls with acrylic gloss varnish in the same manner as with the primer. Note: We suggest using a clear plastic or glass liner if using these bowls for unwrapped foods.

Sources

- Small wood salad and serving bowls are readily available at flea markets, thrift shops, garage sales, and home furnishings and discount stores. You will find round bowls as well as shapes, such as leaves and pineapples.

Painting tip

- Preparing surfaces with white spray primer, such as KILZ, works well for many painting projects. Spray primer works very well on wood, especially if it is dark and light colors of paint are to be used.

Cost to make project

Approximately $1 to $2 per bowl

Suggested selling price

$10 per bowl, $18 for a set of two, and $35 for a set of four.

Time to make project

45 minutes per bowl

Timesaving tips

- In a large, well-ventilated area, lay out several bowls. For priming step, spray several bowls at a time. Use this method for the varnishing step as well.
- Paint one large design in the center of the bowl.

whimsical bowls

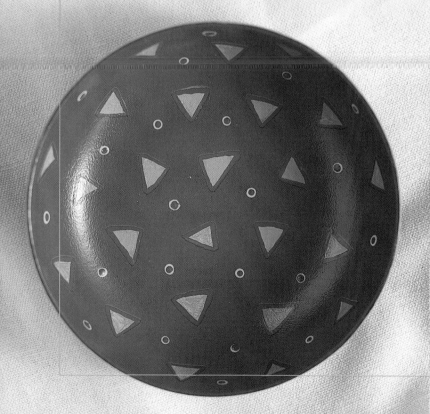

flower pattern

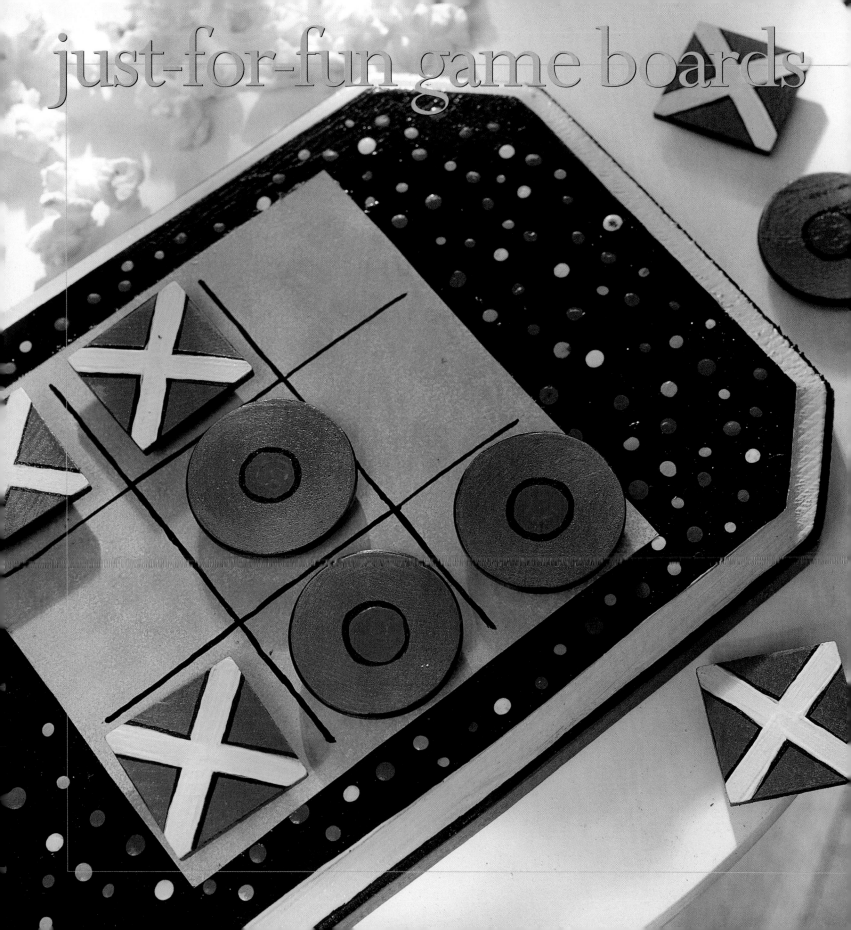

paint it!

Kids of all ages will have fun playing this old-time favorite board game, created by you. These games are easy to put together, leaving you time to dream up different ways to paint each set.

Sources
- Purchase wood crafts boards at discount, crafts, and some home center stores.
- Look for metal sheets in hobby shops, art stores, or home centers.

Cost to make project
Approximately $5 per set

Suggested selling price
$15 to $20, depending on the intricacy of design

Time to make project
1 hour

What you need
Fine sandpaper
Purchased wood crafts board approximately 6¾x9¾ inches
Acrylic paints in desired colors and black
Paintbrushes
Ultra-thin steel
Old scissors
White spray primer
Painting sponge
Thick white crafts glue
5 each of 1½-inch-diameter wood disks
5 each of 1¼-inch wood squares approximately ⅛ inch thick
Clear non-yellowing spray varnish
Ten ¾-inch extra strong magnets

What to do
1. Sand the wood board if needed. Using the photograph, *opposite,* for inspiration, paint the wood piece. Use different colors to accent the grooves and edges, if desired. To make areas stand out, separate them with thin black outlines. Let the paint dry. Add decorative dots by dipping the handle end of a paintbrush into paint and carefully dotting on the surface. Let the paint dry.
2. For game area, cut a 5-inch square of ultra-thin steel with scissors. Spray a light coat of white spray primer onto the metal. Let it dry. Apply a second light coat and let it dry.
3. Sponge-paint the metal piece using a combination of desired colors. Sponge colors together enough to create a soft blend. Do not overdo it; just sponge enough to eliminate the harsh variations of color. Let the paint dry.
4. Glue the metal piece onto the center of the board. Let the glue dry.
5. For square and circular game pieces, paint sides and bottom black. Let dry. Paint tops a base color. Let dry. Paint a black "x" and a black "o." Let dry. Last, add a smaller colored "x" and colored "o" over the black, allowing a black outline to show. Varnish the game pieces. Let dry.
6. Glue magnets to back of game pieces. Let dry.

Painting tip
- DO NOT skip the primer application in Step 2. This is important as it helps the paint bond better to the metal. Spray primer works very well on metal, especially if it is a very slick surface. If you use this primer, you will most likely need fewer coats of paint and the paint also will go on more evenly and smoothly.

Timesaving tips
- Prime several metal pieces at once.
- Use the same color scheme on several game boards to eliminate changing colors of paint.
- Eliminate the metal and magnets and simply paint the square game area in the center of the wood.
- Use a black permanent marker to draw in the lines on the game board.

TO SELL IT
- Take orders for personalized boards, adding $5 to $10 for a custom design.
- Bag the game pieces together so none are lost.
- Use a variety of color combinations when painting the boards so customers can select a set that coordinates with the color scheme in their homes.

TO GIVE IT
- Make a simple drawstring bag from pieces of felt and a shoelace to tie it up.
- For a child, wrap the gift in colorful comics.

There's something magical about these tiny toys. Mesmerize little ones with spinning tops that are inexpensive and quick to make—plus oodles of fun to paint!

21

whirling, twirling tops

daisy

ladybug

lizard

fish

butterfly

geometric

What you need

Pencil
³⁄₁₆-inch dowel
Small saw
Drill with ³⁄₁₆-inch bit
¹⁄₄x2¹⁄₂-inch wood disc
10-millimeter wood beads
Pliers
Fine sandpaper
All-purpose sealer
Fabric transfer paper
Tracing paper
Scissors
Masking tape
Permanent black marker
  or black paint and a
  fine paintbrush
³⁄₄- and 1-inch-diameter
  wood wheels
Paintbrushes
Acrylic paints in desired colors
Wood glue
Drinking glass
Clear spray varnish

What to do

1. Mark and cut dowel into 2¹⁄₂-inch sections. Drill a hole at the center of the disc. While holding bead with pliers, widen one end of hole using the drill.
2. Sand all wood parts. Apply sealer to all pieces and let dry.
3. Cut a 2¹⁄₂-inch circle from transfer paper. Transfer desired design, *opposite*, to tracing paper and cut out circle. Place transfer paper over disc. Place the tracing paper with design over the transfer paper and tape in place. Trace over all lines on the pattern. Remove papers from disc.

4. For designs with black outlines, draw outlines with permanent marker or paint with a fine paintbrush.
5. Fill in the design areas as indicated on the patterns, or choose your own colors. Paint the beads, wheels, and two-thirds of the dowel.
6. To assemble, place the dowel through the center of the disc. Apply glue around the dowel on the wrong side of the disc. Slip on the 1-inch wheel with the flat side facing the disc. Apply glue around the dowel protruding from wheel. Place the ³⁄₄-inch wheel with the flat side facing the 1-inch wheel. Apply a small amount of glue in the bead hole and place on the tip of the dowel. To make sure the top will spin, turn it right side up and rotate slowly to check if the stem is straight.
7. Place top upside down in a drinking glass until the glue is dry. If desired, coat the entire top with clear spray varnish. Let the varnish dry.

Sources
■ Purchase wood supplies and tools at home centers, crafts stores, and discount stores.

Painting tip
■ If paint overlaps the outline, simply draw or paint the outline again, carefully going over the paint.

Cost to make project
Approximately 80¢ per top

Suggested selling price
$5 for one, $9.50 for two.

Time to make project
1½ hours

Timesaving tips
■ Instead of painting these intricate designs, paint freehand designs, splatter-paint, or sponge-paint the pieces.

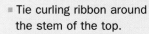

TO SELL IT

■ Show customers how easily they spin and let kids try them out!

TO GIVE IT

■ Tie curling ribbon around the stem of the top.
■ Personalize the design by incorporating a name, phrase, or sentiment. Use a permanent marker to write something such as "Happy Birthday" or "Joe's Top."
■ Tie a personalized top to the bow on a gift.
■ Turn these colorful tops into ornaments by adding a small screw eye at the top and threading with ribbon.

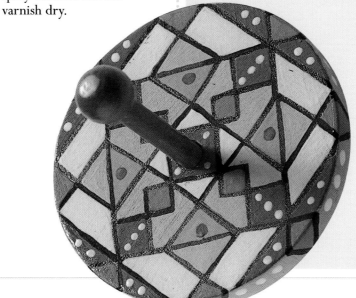

lively lamps

What's hot in home decor? Lighting! Turn ordinary lamps into something special with only two colors of paint and a few easy painting techniques. Add texture with a sponge as well as an array of designs using a paintbrush and a pencil as tools. Use our fun shapes for inspiration or make up your own—the possibilities are endless.

What you need
Lamp and shade
Plastic sandwich bags
Masking tape
Newspapers
White spray primer
Acrylic paints in desired colors
Foam plate
Sea sponge
Paintbrushes
Pencil with round-tip eraser

What to do
1. Before priming the lamp, cover the cord and hardware with plastic sandwich bags. Secure with masking tape.
2. Working in a well-ventilated room, cover your work area with newspapers. Spray both the lamp base and outside of the shade with primer. Let the primer dry.

3. To sponge-paint the base or the shades, put two colors of acrylic paint on a foam plate. Moisten the sponge and dab it into both paint colors. Dab it on the lamp where desired. Continue until the entire section is covered with paint. Let the paint dry.
4. To add painted designs to the base or shade, use the patterns on *pages 26–27* for inspiration. These lamps were painted freehand to achieve a hand-painted look. Paint the designs with the same two colors used for sponging. To make tiny dots, dip the handle end of a paintbrush into paint and dot on the surface. For larger dots, use the eraser tip of a pencil. Let the paint dry.

Sources
- Purchase inexpensive lamps at discount, crafts, and home decor stores. You can also find great buys at flea markets and garage sales. Make sure the wiring is in good shape.

Painting tips
- If you prefer more uniform-size circles for your painted designs, trace the patterns from pages 26–27 onto tracing paper and transfer to the lamp base or shade using transfer paper.
- To paint small dots quickly, you can also use a toothpick, dowel, or skewer dipped in paint. For less regular dots, try using a cotton swab.

Cost to make project
Approximately $5 to $12 per lamp

Suggested selling price
$10 to $35 depending on the size of the lamp and the intricacy of the design

Time to make project
45 minutes

Timesaving tips
- Instead of painting several small designs, paint one large design on the lampshade or base.
- Prime several bases and shades at once.
- Spray-paint the shade using one color and white. Apply in layers, letting them dry between coats. You can mist the entire surface or make large dots by holding the spray can in place just a second or two.

TO SELL IT
- Paint lamps in a variety of sizes and color schemes.
- If electricity is available, plug in a few lamps.
- Wrap the cords with twist ties to keep out of the way.

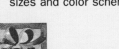

TO GIVE IT
- Wrap up a box of light bulbs to give with the lamp.
- Attach a card with a written sentiment such as, "You light up my life" or "For the bright spot in my life."

lively lamps

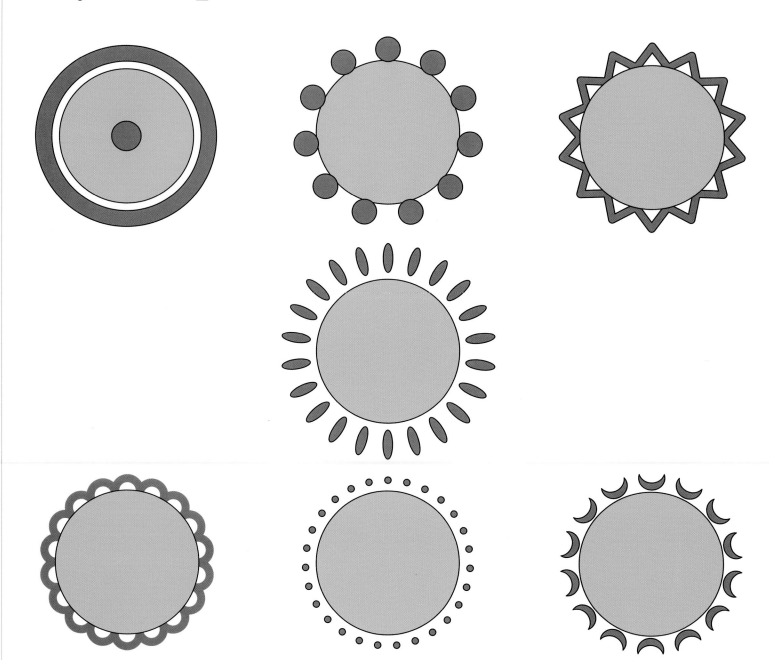

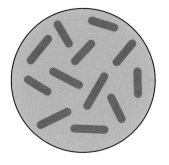
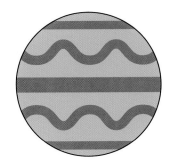
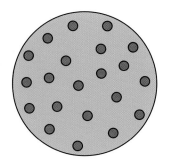

decorative dot patterns

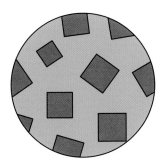
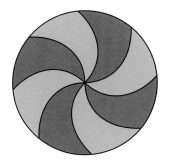

clearly-for-candy jars

*Give these flea market jars
new life by adding
quick-to-make motifs using
glass paints. And because all
the paint remains on the
outside, any kind of goodies
can be placed inside.*

What you need

*Clear glass candy jars
with lids
Tracing paper and pencil
Scissors; masking tape
Glass paints
Paintbrushes
Pencil with round-tip eraser*

What to do

1. Before beginning, wash the glassware and let it dry. Be careful not to touch the areas to be painted.

▶ 2. Using the photographs on *pages 28–29* for inspiration, decide how you want to paint the jars. Most of these designs are painted freehand. To paint the floral jar, *opposite*, trace the pattern below onto tracing paper. Trim any extra paper away from the design. Tape the pattern to the inside of the candy jar. Using a wide flat paintbrush, paint the background stripes. Let dry.

▶ 3. Paint the flower motif, painting over the stripes. Let the paint dry. Add the flower center, leaves, outlines, and highlights. Let the paint dry.

4. To make dots, dip the eraser end of a pencil into paint and dot on the surface of the jar. To paint smaller dots, dip the handle end of a paintbrush into paint.

5. To make small squares, make short strokes using a flat paintbrush. Let the paint dry.

Sources

- Look for candy jars at flea markets, garage sales, crafts, gift, grocery, and discount stores.
- Purchase glass paints at crafts and art stores.

Painting tips

- The glass paint you choose may require baking to become permanent. Be sure to read the paint manufacturer's instructions.
- If layering paint, let each layer dry before painting over it.

Cost to make project

Approximately 50¢ to $1.50 per jar

Suggested selling price

$8 to $15, depending on the size of the jar and the intricacy of the design

Time to make project

½ hour

Timesaving tips

- Paint similarly shaped jars with the same design.
- Make several copies of a traced pattern at a copy center to allow you to work on several jars at once.

TO SELL IT

- Wrap the lids and bottoms separately before bagging.
- Enclose a card with each jar that explains that the paint is permanent but hand washing is recommended.

TO GIVE IT

- Nestle the candy jar in a basket filled with bags and boxes of candies.
- Fill the jar with treats, and tie a bow around the rim or knob on the lid.

floral jar
flower pattern

leaf
pattern
for lid

31

silky sachets

Make lovely sachets from rainbow silk you color. Decorative accents, made with rub-off foil, complete these elegant fringed pillows.

What you need
¾ cup of rice
Plastic sandwich bag with tight closure
Scented oil
Large white scrap paper
Two 6-inch squares of white medium-weight silk fabric
Scissors
Spray bottle of water
Acrylic paints in blue, green, copper, and magenta
Disposable foam plate
Paintbrush
Iron
Pencil

Gold rub-off foil, adhesive, and sealer
28 inches of gold fringe
Straight pins
Sewing machine
Funnel
Needle and thread

What to do
▼ **1.** Pour rice into a plastic bag and add four drops of scented oil. Shake well and keep closed for at least one hour.

continued on page 34

Sources
■ For silk, check remnant section of fabric store for inexpensive scrap fabrics. Also you may use old silk shirts.
■ Scented oils can be found in hobby, craft, discount, grocery, and home decor stores, wherever potpourri is sold.
■ Fine art stores carry acrylic paints created for painting on fabric.

Painting tips
■ The thinner the paint, the easier it will blend together. It will also be more pastel.

■ Some metallic-colored acrylic paints can be purchased for use on fabric.

Cost to make project
Approximately $2.50 per sachet

Suggested selling price
$12 for one sachet, $20 for two

Time to make project
Approximately 1½ hours

Timesaving tip
■ Lay out a large piece of silk, iron it, and draw pencil lines marking 6-inch squares. Then wet it and paint the entire piece of fabric. When dry, cut the fabric squares.

TO SELL IT
■ If selling at a seasonal crafts sale, take advantage of gift-giving holidays, using designs such as hearts for Valentine's Day. Sentiments directed toward specific people, like neighbors, friends, teachers, or grandparents make extra-special gifts.
■ Arrange sachets in pairs of coordinating but not identical colors to encourage multiple purchases.

TO GIVE IT
■ Include one of these elegant sachets when giving clothing, table or bed linens, towels, socks, or scarves.
■ A scarf serves as gift wrap, making two gifts in one. Place the sachet in the center of the scarf and tie the corners together.

33

silky sachets

◀ **2.** Place white paper on flat work surface. Lay the fabric squares on the paper and smooth them out. Spray the fabric squares with water until thoroughly wet but not dripping.

▲ **3.** Place small dabs of paint on a foam plate and thin with water if needed until paint is consistency of light cream. Dip paintbrush in paint and paint onto wet fabric. Paint fabric sections different colors. Dip brush in water and clean well between color changes. Brush the colors together to cover all white surfaces. The paint colors will bleed together. Let fabric dry. Iron smooth if needed.

moon-and-star pattern

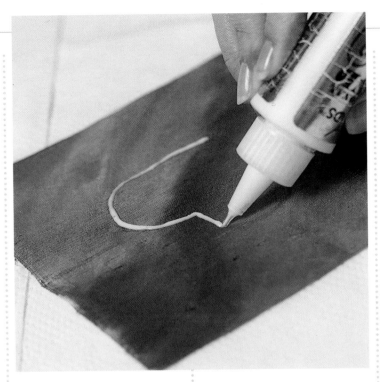

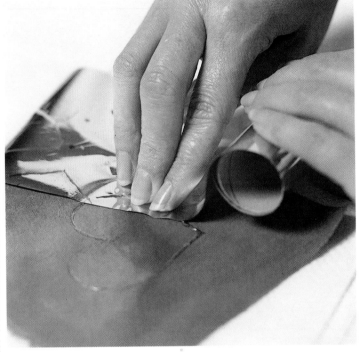

▲ **4.** To add the gold design, draw any simple design you wish with a pencil at least 1¼ inches from the edge. You can use the patterns *below* and *opposite*, or draw your own design or letter. Draw over the pencil line with adhesive. It will appear milky but will dry clear. The glue should be tacky, but firm enough to not smear when touched.

▲ **5.** Place the gold foil sheet over the adhesive with right side up. Rub gently with fingers over the gold foil, leaving the foil on the adhesive design. Pull away the excess. Paint over the gold foil with clear sealer that comes with the gold rub-off foil.

6. Lay one finished square of fabric with the right side up. Pin the gold trim along the edge with the raw edges together. Sew the trim close to the edge of the fabric square.

7. Place the remaining finished square on top of first square with the right sides together. Pin the two layers together. Sew the pieces using a ½-inch seam, leaving a 1½-inch opening along one side.

8. Turn the pillow right side out. Pour the scented rice into the sachet bag until filled as desired. Using a funnel may make this process easier. Hand-sew the opening shut using a needle and thread.

heart pattern

crazy crackled frames

New or recycled, painted frames bring sunshine to any room. These funky versions use a crackle medium to let the vivid colors peek through.

What you need

Wood picture frame
Newspapers
White spray primer
Acrylic paints in desired colors and white
Paintbrushes
Crackle medium
Acrylic sealer
Glass cleaner
Soft rag or paper towel

What to do

1. Remove the backing and glass from the frame. Set them aside.

2. In a well-ventilated area, cover the work surface with newspapers. Spray the picture frame with primer paint. Let the paint dry.

3. Paint the base coat using colorful acrylic paints. You can blend the colors together or paint stripes. (The base-coat colors of paint will show through the cracks after the crackle medium and top coat of paint are applied.) Let the paint dry.

4. Read the directions on the label of the crackle medium. Apply a coat of the crackle medium. For fine cracks, the instructions will usually say to apply a thin coat. For thicker, more noticeable cracks, paint on two coats, letting it dry between coats. Let the crackle medium dry.

5. Paint the top coat of white paint by covering the entire frame or by painting stripes as shown. To achieve the crackled appearance, try to paint the top coat with single strokes, without repainting over any areas. Repainting can cause the paint to pull up and the crackle effect can be lost. Let the paint dry.

6. Add checked borders, if desired, using a small flat paintbrush. Let the paint dry.

7. Apply a coat of acrylic sealer. Let the sealer dry.

8. Carefully wash the glass that was removed from the frame. Let it dry. Place the glass into the frame. Insert the desired photograph or artwork. Replace the backing to secure.

Sources

- Purchase frames at discount, crafts, and home decor stores as well as flea markets and home improvement centers.
- Crackle medium is available in paint, discount, crafts, and art stores.

Painting tips

- Before painting the frame, practice using the crackle medium. When applying the top coat over the crackle medium, avoid repainting over any strokes to prevent pulling up the paint and losing the crackle effect.
- When using spray paint of any kind, be sure the area is well ventilated and the work surface is protected from overspray.

Cost to make project
$1 to $2.50 per frame

Suggested selling price
$6 to $24 per frame

Time to make project
Approximately 25 minutes

Timesaving tips

- Prime and apply sealer to several frames at once.
- Use the same color combinations on several frames and complete in an assembly-line fashion.
- Avoid frames that use nails to hold glass, backing, and photographs or art in place. Choose frames that have sliding pieces that slip over the backing piece to secure frame contents.

TO SELL IT

- Make coordinating frames in various sizes to encourage buying sets.
- When displaying frames, mount a variety of items within the frames—leaves, photos, medals, children's drawings, etc.

TO GIVE IT

- Frame a personal message for the recipient.
- Photocopy snapshots of family members or friends to make wrapping paper for the frames.

pushpin pals

Imagine these adorable characters helping keep clutter to a minimum! Concealing a pushpin, our barnyard of miniature animals would love to gather on any size corkboard.

What you need
Waxed paper
Acrylic paints in white, brown, terra-cotta, yellow, orange, gray, black, and pink
Small paintbrushes
Micro wood flowerpots
Tracing paper and pencil
Crafting foam sheets in yellow, white, brown, orange, flesh, pink, and rust
Small scissors
Tack
Thick white crafts glue
Paper punch
3/8-inch bell
3-millimeter wiggly eyes
5-millimeter brown pom-poms

What to do
1. Cover work area with waxed paper. Paint the base color on miniature pots for heads. Paint additional coats if needed. Let the paint dry.

Paint the details, spots, stripes, etc., using the photo, *opposite*, as a guide.
2. Trace foam patterns, *below*, onto tracing paper. Transfer shapes to foam sheets and cut out all pieces. Puncture a hole in the center of each foam shape using a tack.
3. Place a small amount of glue inside the wood flowerpot, insert the tack base, and continue filling with glue until level with the rim.
4. Push backing foam centered on tack against the rim of the pot. Place the base down on waxed paper to dry. (Glue may leak from the hole in the base of the pot.)
5. Glue the pieces and trims as shown, *opposite*. Let dry.

Sources
- Purchase miniature wood flowerpots and crafting foam at crafts and discount stores.
- Look for pushpins at discount, office supply, and art stores.

Painting tip
- You may find it more efficient to use spray paint for the background colors.

Cost to make project
25¢ to 50¢ each

Suggested selling price
$1 per pin, all eight for $7.50

Time to make project
Approximately 30 minutes per pushpin

Timesaving tips
- Make several of each animal in stages.
- Rather than painting on the details, draw them in with permanent marker.

TO SELL IT
- Push each pin into a small cork to avoid injury.
- Neatly arrange a small bulletin board using each of the pushpin designs.

TO GIVE IT
- Push a collection of pins into a small corkboard and attach a personal message or two for the recipient.
- Make one of the characters without a pushpin and glue it to the front of a gift tag.

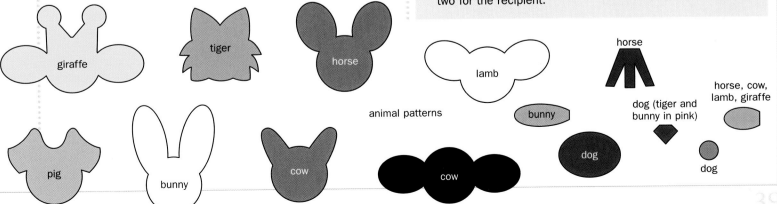

animal patterns

WITH
NEEDLE
AND
THREAD

Sewn treasures, whether heirloom or newly made,

always entice shoppers with their lovingly stitched details.

This chapter honors a variety of sewing techniques with

a treasury of timeless projects, easy enough for even

a beginner to master. So choose your favorite project,

find your sewing basket, and start stitching showstopper

creations with needle and thread.

SEW A FINE SEAM

Making Projects with Needle and Thread

The key elements in successful sewing are to take the time to carefully cut patterns, stitch straight lines, clip corners, and trim thread ends. Once you've mastered the basics, you'll begin to sew faster and smarter—without sacrificing quality or consistency.

Keeping your work area tidy will help keep projects moving along efficiently and reduce the risk of errors. There's nothing more frustrating than knowing you have the perfect trims for a project but you cannot find them.

If your project requires embroidery stitches, such as French knots or buttonhole stitches, practice on a scrap piece of fabric until you feel confident. When you're ready, you'll be able to embellish your projects with ease.

When purchasing materials for sewing, watch for sales at your local fabric and crafts shops. Stock up on such items as fabric, felt, ribbon, and buttons when they are advertised at a discount.

Selling Sewn Items

Keeping items clean and neat is key when selling products made of fabric. When storing or transporting your lovingly made items, wrap them in plain white tissue to avoid getting any dirt on the surface. You may need to bring an iron to your show to touch up any projects that have been badly creased. And remember scissors in case you discover a loose thread.

Attach price tags to sewn projects with embroidery floss sewn directly to the item, or attach the floss to a safety pin and secure it that way. Make sure the pen used to price the item is permanent so the ink does not rub off. Keep all pens and pencils away from the sewn creations so they don't leave unwanted marks.

If your sewn item has special care instructions, such as washing, drying, dry cleaning, etc., note this on the price tag or a separate care sheet. Enclose a business card with every purchase so customers can call you if they have questions on how to care for their sewn items. This also is a good way to get repeat business and special orders.

Many sewn projects are for home decor—pillows, quilts, table linens—so it's wise to make items using a variety of fabrics. When setting up your space at a show, group the coordinating fabrics and colors to encourage multiple sales.

For small projects, such as eyeglass cases, you may want to fill a few to make your display interesting. Other items may require a label so the customers know as much as possible about what they are considering purchasing. For instance, if making and selling the basket liners, *pages 46–47*, you may want to record the size of the basket and a few items that fit inside (CDs, paper napkins, guest towels, etc.).

mending jars

Not just for jelly, these petite canning jars are cleverly transformed into organizers for mending necessities—such as buttons, needles, and thread.

What you need
Pencil
4-ounce canning jar with lid and band
3x3-inch piece of 1-inch-thick foam
Scissors
Thread and needle
5-inch circle of calico fabric
2x2-inch piece of felt
Pinking shears
Thick white crafts glue
2¼x1¼-inch piece of card stock paper
Felt scraps
Items to fill jar, such as buttons, needles, thread, thimble, safety pins, etc.
18 inches of ⅛-inch-wide satin ribbon
Sew-through button
½-inch gold sewing charm

What to do
1. Trace the widest part of the band circle onto foam; cut out. Using thread, gather the outside edge of the calico circle. Place the circle of foam onto the top of the lid. Add the calico circle, pulling the gathers tight on the underside, and allowing a ¾-inch opening. Cut a 1½-inch circle of felt with pinking shears.

2. Glue the felt over the gathered fabric on the underside of the lid. Smooth the calico over the foam, pushing the foam away slightly at the lid edge. Add the band.

3. To make the thread and needle holder, cut card stock paper on the long sides using pinking shears. On one short side, stitch a piece of felt that is pinked on all sides and slightly larger than the card stock. Allow ⅜ inch of felt to fold over the end of the card stock.

4. Machine-stitch across one end of the felt, securing the card stock.

5. Wrap an assortment of thread on the card stock. Add safety pins at the stitched edge. Insert two needles under the thread into stitched edge.

6. Fill the jar with desired sewing notions. Tie the ribbon around the jar rim. Thread a button and a gold charm onto the ribbon. Tie the ribbon ends into a bow.

Sources
- Canning jars are available in several designs and sizes and can be purchased at thrift shops or discount, home decor, grocery, or crafts stores.

Sewing and finishing tips
- To add your "signature" to each jar, glue on a personalized sewing tag under the lid.
- If you don't have pinking shears, trim the edge of the circle with rickrack or other decorative trim.

- To put a monogram on the top of the jar cover, cross-stitch gingham fabric instead of using calico.

Cost to make project
Approximately $2

Suggested selling price
$9 for one jar

Time to make project
25 minutes

Timesaving tip
- Cut several calico and felt circles at once by layering fabrics before cutting.

TO SELL IT
- Display some of the jars using the gift-giving ideas, *below.*
- Use a variety of calico and felt colors.
- Display a sign that reads,

"Great idea for a secret pal or teacher!"
- Wrap the jars in bubble wrap to avoid breakage.
- Use an old sewing machine, sewing basket, and packaged patterns for props in the display.

TO GIVE IT
- Wrap a mending jar with a beginner's how-to-sew book for a student traveling to college.
- For the cross-stitcher, fill the jar with tapestry

needles and skeins of embroidery floss.
- Fill the jar with colorful beads and use the pincushion top to hold a pair of beading needles.

bow-tied basket liners

Baskets are ever-special when lined with colorful fitted fabric. Here you'll find a simple formula for adjusting the liner size to fit just about any square or rectangular basket.

What you need
Basket
Tape measure
Square or rectangular basket
1 yard of fabric
Straight pins
¼ yard of contrasting fabric
Rickrack or other desired trim
Needle and thread

What to do
1. Measure the outside of the basket for width, length, and height as shown *below*. For the main fabric measurement, add two times the height plus the width to equal the cutting-width measurement. Add two times the height plus the length to equal the cutting-length measurement. Cut the fabric to this size.
2. For the liner, fold the fabric on the bias. From one corner, measure the height. Mark and pin this point. Check the fit and make any necessary adjustments. Stitch from the mark to a right angle to the fold. Repeat for all four corners. Trim seam allowance to ¼ inch.
3. For the fold-over cuff, cut two pieces of contrasting fabric

that each measure half the height and half the circumference of the basket top. Cut two pieces from the main fabric that are 1 inch wider. Place a contrasting fabric piece over a main fabric piece with right sides facing. Stitch one long side on each pair using a ½-inch seam. Press. Fold pieces lengthwise with right sides facing. Stitch across the ends. Trim the corners. Turn to the right side. If desired, stitch decorative trim over seam where fabrics meet.
4. Baste the cuff from handle to handle with right sides facing. Stitch. Press cuff to right side.
5. To make the fabric ties, cut two pieces 28x3½ inches. Fold lengthwise with right sides facing. Stitch, tapering to a point at ends and leaving an opening for turning. Turn. Stitch closed. Press. Tack ties to the sides of the liner. Tie the bows around the handle.

Sources
■ Look for baskets in flea markets and garage sales, as well as discount, import, home decor, and crafts stores.

Sewing and finishing tips
■ For a basket without a handle, adjust the cuff to be a continuous strip.
■ Once you've mastered this liner process, add a ruffle to the cuff.

Cost to make project
$3 to $10 including basket

Suggested selling price
$9 to $20 per basket

Time to make project
½ hour

Timesaving tips
■ Instead of sewing fabric strips to make bows, use a wide ribbon.
■ Layer fabrics and cut several fabric pieces at once.

TO SELL IT
■ Post a list of uses, such as a magazine holder, sewing basket, organizer, etc.
■ Display a variety of basket shapes and sizes with interchangeable liners (some seasonal) to encourage multiple sales.

TO GIVE IT
■ Fill the basket with inspiring reading material, get-well items for a friend who is ill, fresh fruit, or hobby supplies.
■ Make a coordinating set for someone who has a home office.

little hen pincushions

Keep pins and needles sharp and handy with these adorable hens that do it all. Made from scraps of calico fabric, felt, and embroidery floss, these colorful pincushions come to the rescue for anyone who loves to sew.

What you need

Tracing paper
Pencil
Scissors
6x12-inch piece of fusible interfacing
6x12-inch piece of calico fabric for body
Iron
6x4-inch piece of contrasting calico for wings
6x4-inch piece of coordinating felt for wing lining
6x6-inch piece of fusible web paper
3x3-inch piece of red felt for comb and wattle
2x2-inch piece of green felt for emery bag
3x4-inch piece of mat board for base
10-inch piece of medium rickrack
Polyester fiberfill
Yellow-orange and green embroidery floss
Needle
Two tiny black buttons
Thread

What to do

1. Trace the pattern pieces, *pages 50–51,* onto tracing paper and cut out.
2. Iron the interfacing to the wrong side of the calico. Cut two body pieces (reversing one), adding a ½-inch seam allowance. Trace the wing pieces (reversing one) onto fusible web paper. Cut out and iron to the felt for the wing lining. Cut the felt slightly bigger than the wing. Machine-stitch the details on the wing. Topstitch the wing to each body side leaving open at the top edge to create a pocket.
3. Iron two layers of the red felt together for the comb. Use the pattern to cut the comb. Cut the wattle from a single piece of red felt. Cut the emery top from green felt.
4. Cut one base from the mat board and fusible web paper. Sandwich fusible web paper between the calico and the mat board. Iron in place. Cut out calico,

continued on page 50

Sources

- Look for fabric in discount, crafts, fabric, and quilting stores.
- Purchase needle holders, thimbles, and other sewing supplies in crafts, discount, fabric, quilting, and needlework stores.

Sewing and finishing tips

- You can recycle old linens to create one-of-a-kind sewing hens.
- All details can be added with embroidery stitches, if desired.

TO SELL IT

- Place a sign by hens with ideas for recipients: away-from-home students, aunts, grandmothers, daughters, teachers, etc.
- Use old chicken crates as tables to display the hens.
- Fill a basket with wooden or blown-out brown eggs and put the chickens in the basket. Give an egg as a bonus when buying a pincushion.

TO GIVE IT

- Nest a hen in a small sewing basket filled with such items as pins, needles, safety pins, and spools of thread.
- Cut the bottom off a half-dozen egg carton, place hen in carton, and wrap with cellophane.

Cost to make project
Approximately $3

Suggested selling price
$12 to $14

Time to make project
1 hour

Timesaving tips
- Delete wing details and emery bag.
- Layer fabrics to cut several pieces at once.
- Set up an assembly line, having someone fill the chickens with fiberfill, someone adding the details, etc.

adding ½ inch all around. Clip the seam allowance and iron to the wrong side of the mat board.

5. Stitch the body pieces together with right sides facing and leaving the bottom edge open. Clip the seam. Turn to the right side.

6. Turn under the bottom edge on the fold line and baste. Topstitch rickrack around the bottom edge. Stuff the body. Whipstitch the bottom with mat board to bottom edge of body adding stuffing as necessary.

7. Embroider the beak using satin stitches. Add buttons for eyes. Whipstitch the wattle and the comb in place.

8. For the needle sharpener emery bag, use the pattern, *right*, to cut the piece from contrasting fabric. Fold in half with the wrong sides facing and stitch as shown. Stuff with fiberfill. Gather around the top edge. Poke a hole in the center of the felt top. Attach floss to the body; thread on the felt emery bag topper, and then the emery bag. Glue the felt over the gathered part of the emery bag.

wattle pattern
(cut one)

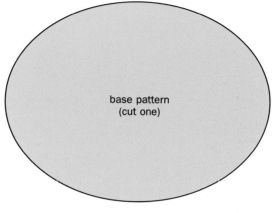

base pattern
(cut one)

emery bag topper pattern
(cut one)

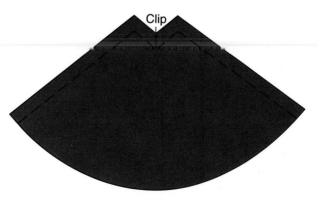

Clip

emery bag pattern
(cut one)

beak
satin stitch

crown pattern
(cut two)

wing pattern
(cut two, reversing one)

fold line

body pattern
(cut two, reversing one)

hen pincushion
placement diagram

snazzy spec cases

With a rainbow of felt colors available, make these delightful glasses cases in all your favorite color combinations. Use your imagination to add a variety of felt shapes and specialty-stitch details to the case fronts.

What you need
Pencil
Tracing paper
Scissors
Felt in desired colors
Pins
Embroidery floss in desired colors

What to do
1. Trace the patterns, *pages 54–55*, for the desired eyeglass case onto tracing paper. Cut out the patterns. Cut the pieces from felt colors of choice (we used black, fuchsia, blue, purple, and red).

2. For the bow case, lay the largest felt piece flat. Pin the large strip atop it as shown. Using blanket stitches as shown on *page 54* and three plies of floss, sew the two pieces together at the edges. Fold the case in half with right sides out.

Sew the sides closed using three plies of floss and blanket stitches. To add French knot dots to the small bow shape, use six plies of desired colors of embroidery floss. Sew to the larger bow shape using blanket stitches. Wrap the center of the bow with embroidery floss. Tack the bow to the top of the eyeglass case.

3. For the diamond case, sew the circle to the center of the diamond using blanket stitches and embroidery floss. Sew the diamond to the next largest felt shape using blanket stitches, centering it on one half of the large piece. Pin this felt piece to the remaining large piece, sewing together using blanket stitches. Sew the bottom and side closed using blanket stitches. Use embroidery floss to wrap the corner where the case meets the bow.

Sources
- Purchase felt in sheets (approximately 8x11 or 11x17 inches) or by the yard at fabric, discount, and crafts stores. Purchase large sheets or by-the-yard lengths for this project. The small accent pieces can be cut from small sheets or scraps of felt.

Sewing and finishing tips
- Use a sharp, large-eyed needle when sewing with six plies of embroidery floss. Use fewer plies for finer details.
- Before purchasing felt, check the quality. Some felts are very thin. For this project, select thick, dense pieces of felt.

Cost to make project
$1 to $1.50 per case

Suggested selling price
$8 to $12 depending on intricacy of details

Time to make project
45 minutes

Timesaving tips
- Buy felt by the yard and cut several cases at once.
- Replace French knots with seed beads.
- Add buttons or beads to the outside of the glasses holder instead of using specialty stitches.

TO SELL IT
- Stuff the cases slightly to give them some dimension.
- Display with reading glasses and sunglasses.
- Arrange cases in baskets lined with shredded mylar.

TO GIVE IT
- For someone who wears glasses, place the case on a book, tie with ribbon, and add a tag that reads "Happy Reading."
- Slip a pair of colorful sunglasses in the case before giving to a friend.

snazzy spec cases

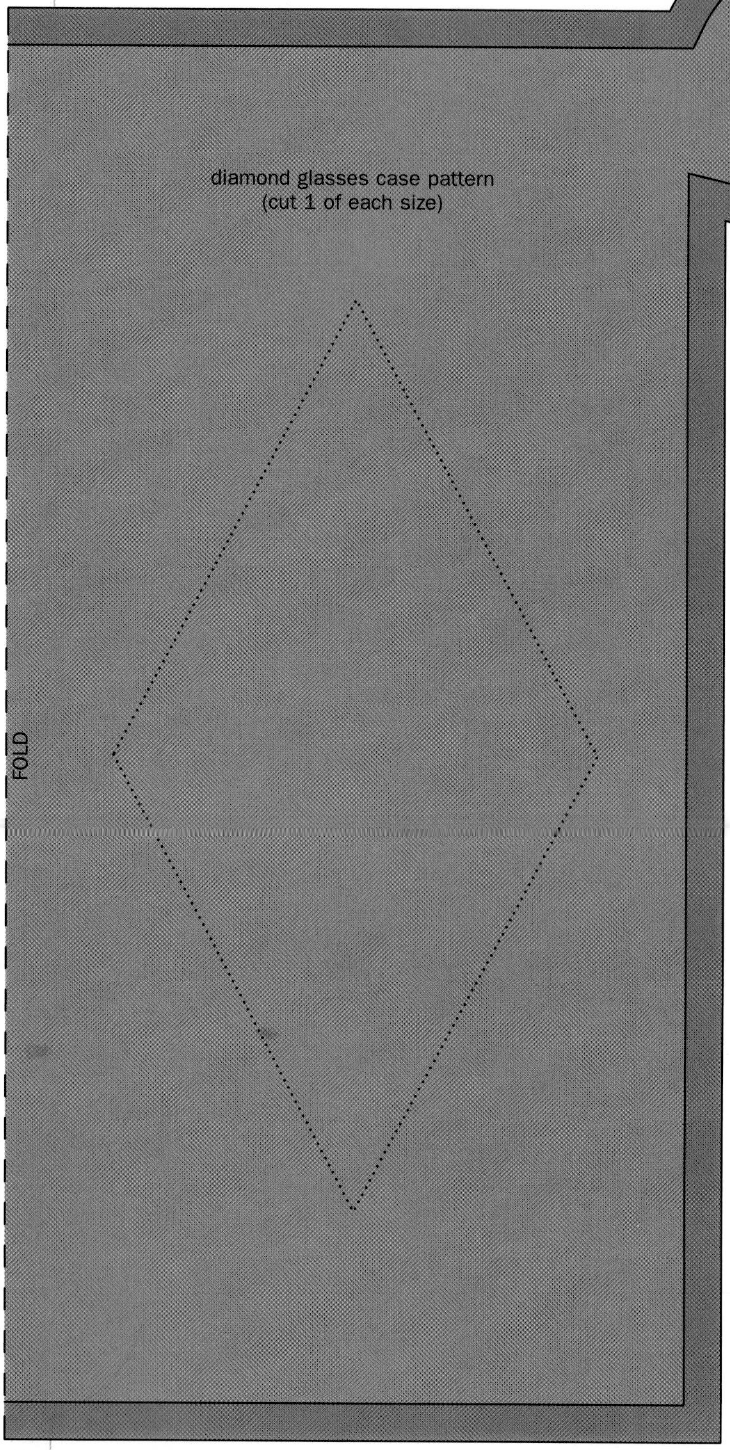

diamond glasses case pattern
(cut 1 of each size)

FOLD

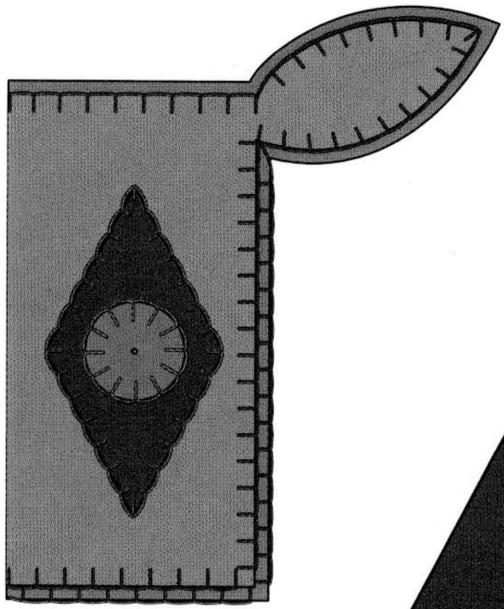

diamond glasses
case placement
diagram

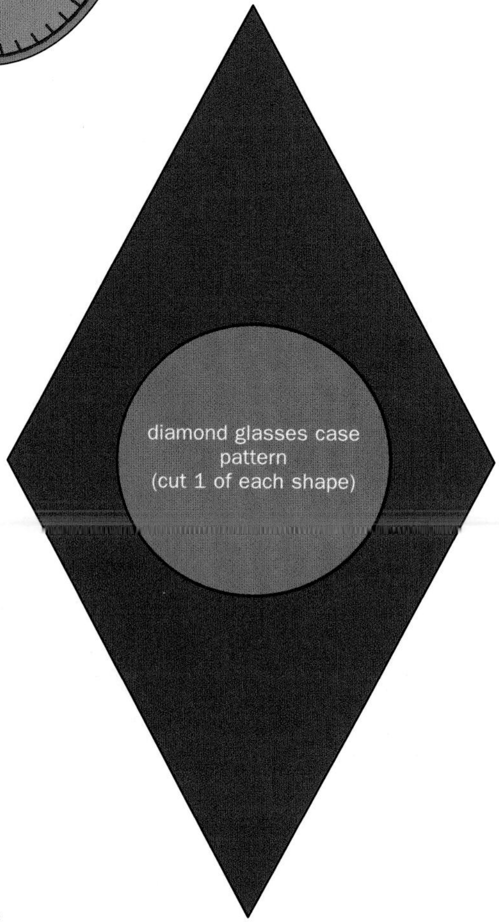

diamond glasses case
pattern
(cut 1 of each shape)

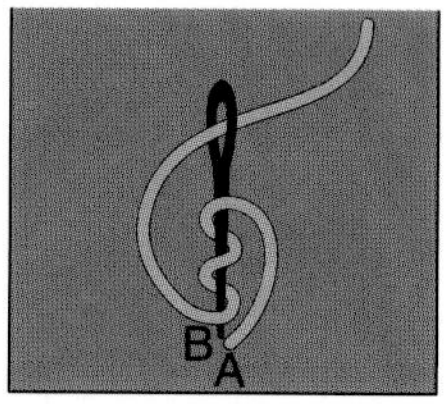

french knot

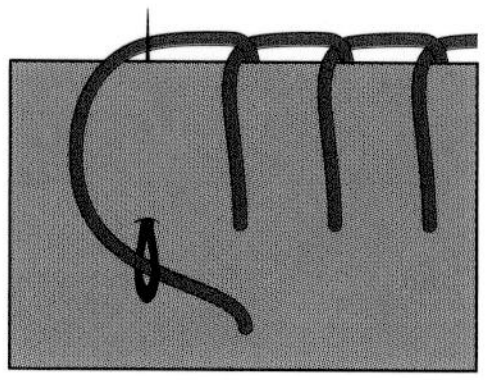

blanket stitch

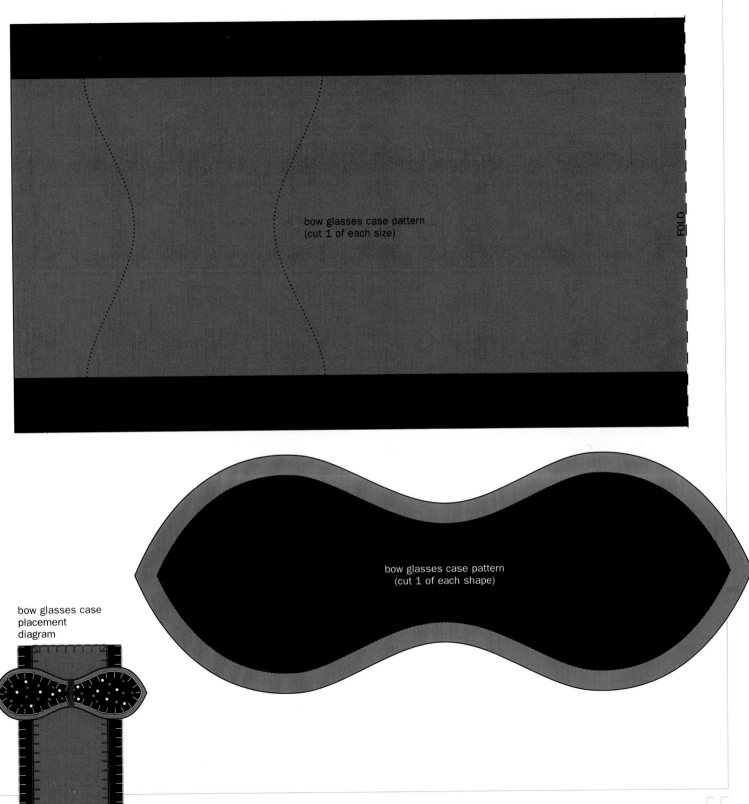

bow glasses case pattern
(cut 1 of each size)

FOLD

bow glasses case pattern
(cut 1 of each shape)

bow glasses case
placement
diagram

so-cool hot pads

Checks and calicos add vintage flavor to these easy-to-make hot pads. The ladybug has button spots, while the other hot pad holds crushed cinnamon sticks and cloves for an aromatic bonus.

Sources
- Purchase fabrics and sewing notions at fabric, discount, and crafts stores. For an authentic vintage appearance, look for fabrics in antiques stores, flea markets, and garage sales.

Sewing and finishing tips
- Use trims other than rickrack, such as grosgrain ribbon or braid.
- For a country look, use embroidery floss to attach the buttons, knotting floss on the right side of the button and trimming the ends short.

Cost to make project
$1.50

Suggested selling price
$5 for one, $9 for a matching pair

Time to make project
½ hour per hot pad

Timesaving tips
- Layer fabrics and cut several hot pads at once.
- For the four-patch hot pad, use a single circle instead of piecing the background fabric. Delete the spice mixture if desired.

ladybug hot pad

What you need
Two 8-inch circles of checked fabric
8-inch circle of extra-loft fleece
Straight pins
¼ yard of jumbo black rickrack
Needle and thread
4x7-inch piece of black fabric
Scissors
1 yard of extra-wide double-fold black bias tape
Eight ⅝-inch black buttons

What to do
1. Layer and pin the back checked circle, fleece, and front checked circle. Topstitch rickrack through the center of the fabrics.
2. Fold the black fabric in half lengthwise and pin to layered fabrics using the photograph, *opposite*, as a guide. Trim the raw edges even with the circle. Remove the straight pins.
3. Bind the outside edge with bias tape, adding a loop for hanging. Stitch buttons on each side of the rickrack to make the dots on the ladybug.

spiced hot pad

What you need
5x5-inch square each of four different checked fabrics
Fusible web paper
5-inch circle of calico fabric for center front circle 8-inch circle of calico fabric for the back
8-inch circle of extra-loft fleece
Crushed cinnamon sticks and cloves; needle and thread
¾ yard of maxi rickrack for binding
½ yard of jumbo rickrack for front circle

What to do
1. With right sides facing, stitch the checked fabrics into a four-patch, using a ¼-inch seam allowance. Center and fuse the 5-inch calico circle to the four-patch.
2. Layer calico back, fleece (sprinkled with crushed cinnamon sticks and cloves), and pieced circle. Baste the layers together at the edge.
3. Bind the edge with maxi rickrack. Topstitch jumbo rickrack around the small circle.

TO SELL IT
- Display a "guess my scent" sign by the spiced hot pads.
- Tie coordinating or matching sets together to encourage customers to buy hot pads in sets of two.

TO GIVE IT
- Give a pair of hot pads along with your favorite cookie, bread, veggie, or casserole recipe.
- Roll up a set of hot pads. Wrap with tissue paper, tying with a ribbon bow on each end.

fun felt pillows

To quickly change the look of a room, new throw pillows may be the solution! These small square pillows made from felt are sure to add a ray of sunshine, whether displayed alone or in a grouping.

fun felt pillows

What you need for all of the pillows
Pencil and tracing paper
Scissors
Straight pins
Fiberfill
No. 20 chenille needle

penny pillow

What you need
Scraps of felt in neon yellow, fuchsia, lime, emerald green, and turquoise
¹⁄₃ yard of camel felt
Dark emerald green embroidery floss

What to do
1. Trace the circle patterns from *page 63* onto tracing paper and cut out. Cut 16 large and 16 small circles from the assorted felts. Cut three to four of each color. Cut two 12x12-inch pieces from camel felt.

2. Stack the small circles centered on top of contrasting colored large circles. Stitch the circles together with straight stitches around the edge of the small circle. Use three plies of floss for all stitches.
3. Arrange a square of the stitched circles, four rows of four, centered on one piece of the camel felt. Pin in place. Stitch the circles to the camel felt using straight stitches.

heart pillow

What you need
6x6-inch pieces of felt in neon lime and fuchsia
¹⁄₃ yard of green felt
Light cranberry embroidery floss

What to do
1. Trace the "frame" and heart patterns from *page 62* onto tracing paper and cut out. Cut one frame shape from neon lime felt, one heart from fuchsia felt, and two 12x12-inch pieces from green felt.
2. Center the frame on one green square. Pin in place and stitch with straight stitches around the outside and inside edges. Use three plies of floss for all stitches. Pin the heart centered inside the open frame. Stitch with straight stitches.

woven square pillow

What you need
19x12-inch piece of felt in fuchsia and emerald green
¹⁄₃ yard of camel felt
Dark blue-violet embroidery floss

What to do
1. Cut four 6x1¹⁄₂-inch strips from fuchsia and emerald green felt. Cut two 12x12-inch pieces from camel felt.
2. Lay the fuchsia strips side by side. Weave a square, weaving over and under using the green strips. Pin the woven square centered onto one camel felt piece. Using three plies of floss, stitch the pieces together using straight stitches, *page 63*, around the outside edges of the woven square.

square in diamond pillow

What you need

19x12-inch piece of felt in emerald green and yellow
1/3 yard of turquoise felt
Fuchsia embroidery floss
1-inch pink heart button

What to do

1. Cut one 5½x5½-inch square from emerald green felt, one 8½x8½-inch square from yellow, and two 12x12-inch squares from turquoise.
2. With the yellow square turned on point, pin the green square centered on the yellow piece as shown,

below. Using three plies of embroidery floss, stitch the felt pieces together using blanket stitches.
3. Pin the yellow and green felt unit on top of the turquoise square with the yellow piece turned on point. Stitch together with blanket stitches.
4. Sew the heart button in the center of the green square. Clip the threads.

How to finish all pillows

1. Pin the completed pillow front to the remaining 12-inch square of felt. Stitch the front to the back with blanket stitches, using three plies of the embroidery floss in the color used for the other stitching on the pillow. Leave a 10-inch opening on one side.
2. Through the opening, stuff the pillow with fiberfill. Continue with blanket stitches to sew the opening closed.

Sources

- Purchase felt at fabric or crafts stores.
- The fiberfill and floss can be purchased from discount, crafts, fabric, and stitchery stores.

Sewing and finishing tips

- For other decorative pillow patterns, try tracing around cookie cutters with simple motifs. Then cut from felt.
- Circular pillows can be made using these same basic techniques.

Cost to make project

$2.50 to $3 per pillow

Suggested selling price

$12 to $15 depending on the intricacy of the pillow design

Time to make project

3 hours per pillow

Timesaving tip

- Some handstitches can be replaced by machine sewing, if desired.

TO SELL IT

- Make pillows in a variety of colors to go with any decor.
- Attach a price tag to embroidery floss, then attach to the pillow using a safety pin.
- You may want to have special order forms available for customers
- to order pillows in specific colors.
- Make care tags that recommend the pillows be dry-cleaned.
- Display a sign reminding customers to remember teachers, aunts, grandmas, babysitters, coworkers, friends, and Sunday school teachers and staff.

TO GIVE IT

- These pillows make great housewarming, wedding, and birthday gifts.
- Place a set of pillows in a solid coordinating pillowcase and tie with a bow.

fun felt pillows

heart pillow patterns
(cut one of each)

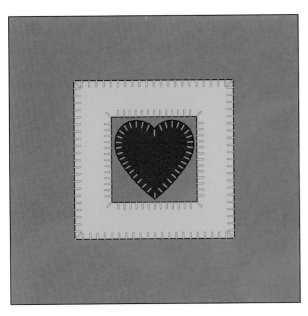

heart pillow placement diagram

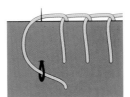

blanket stitch

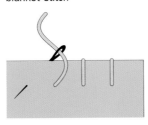

straight stitch

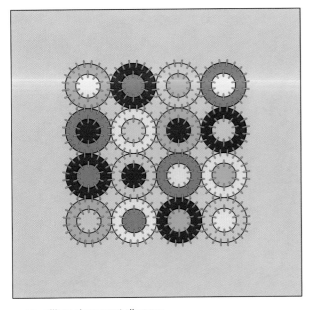

penny pillow placement diagram

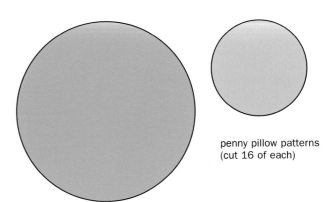

penny pillow patterns
(cut 16 of each)

merry mittens

No one will mind bundling up for the cold with these delightful mittens to keep hands warm. With a dozen ideas to inspire you, each pair you make could be one-of-a-kind.

See page 69 for mitten construction instructions

What you need for all mittens

*Tracing paper and pencil
Fusible web paper; scissors
½ yard each of mitten and lining fabrics (see variation)
Two 6½x6½-inch pieces of cuff fabric (see variation)
20 inches of ¼-inch-wide elastic*

heart or star mittens

What you need

*Print corduroy for mitten fabric; lining fabric; fleece for cuff
4x4-inch piece of imitation cloth suede, such as Ultrasuede, for heart or star
1½x1½-inch pieces of Ultrasuede, in six different colors for circles
Embroidery floss in desired colors*

continued on page 67

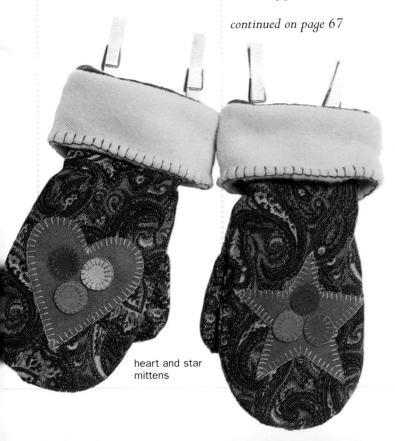

heart and star mittens

Sources
- Look for imitation cloth suede, available in vibrant colors, in fabric stores.
- Available in fabric and crafts stores, fusible web paper is thin enough to see through when tracing a pattern.

Sewing and finishing tip
- To create interest when sewing on the buttons, sew on a 4-hole button by making a square with your stitches, or on a 2-hole button, sew from the center holes to the outside as shown, opposite.

Cost to make project
$3 to $6 per pair of mittens

Suggested selling price
$18 to $24 per pair of mittens

Time to make project
1½ to 2 hours

Timesaving tips
- Cut several mittens from fabric and construct them in stages.
- When enlarging a pattern that is on a grid, take the pattern to a copy center. The pattern on page 68 must be enlarged until one square equals 1 inch.

TO SELL IT
- If space allows, use clothespins to display several mitten styles on a rope.
- Be sure to include care instructions with each pair of mittens sold.
- To display mittens standing up, stuff with tissue paper or fiberfill and stand them up on the cuffs.
- Make sure pairs of mittens don't get separated. Attach them together by sewing a length of floss through the cuffs and a price tag too.

TO GIVE IT
- As a fun surprise, tuck a gift certificate inside one of the mittens.
- For someone young at heart, give a pair of mittens along with the makings for a snowman—buttons for the eyes and mouth, a carrot for the nose, and a fabric scrap for the scarf.

merry mittens

star mitten
pattern

snowman
mitten pattern

snowflake
mitten pattern

heart mitten
pattern

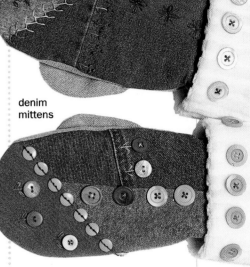

denim
mittens

ribbon-trimmed mittens

What you need
Green wool for mitten fabric; lining fabric; plaid corduroy for cuff
½ yard each of four different ribbons ½–⅝ inch wide

What to do
1. For woven ribbon mittens, see the photo *below* as a guide, and weave four ribbons on each mitten front. Topstitch in place.
2. For tailored bow mittens, *below*, overlap the ends of a 6-inch piece of ribbon. Hand-stitch so the seam is centered at the bottom. Cover the center front and back seam with same color

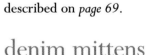

ribbon and stitch in place.
3. Assemble the mittens as described on *page 69*.

denim mittens

What you need
Pieces of denim or jeans for mitten fabric; lining fabric; fleece for cuff
Sew-through buttons
Cotton embroidery floss

What to do
1. Make a two three-piece patchworks from denim, allowing enough fabric for mitten fronts.
2. Trim where desired using embroidery floss and specialty stitches such as feather, lazy daisy, French knot, blanket, and straight stitches. Add buttons where desired.
3. Assemble the mittens as described on *page 69*.

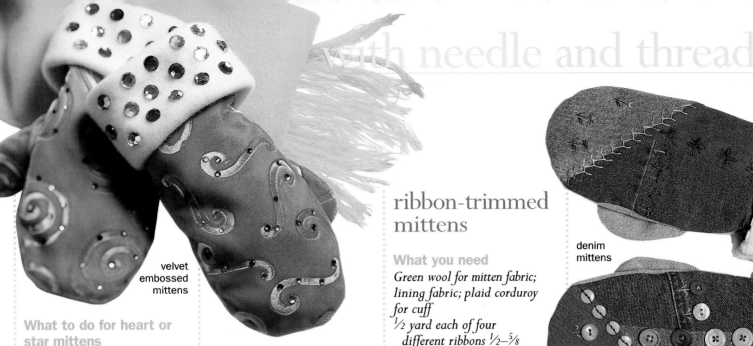

velvet
embossed
mittens

What to do for heart or star mittens

(shown on page 65)
1. Trace heart or star, and six circles, *opposite,* onto fusible web paper. Fuse to corresponding imitation suede. Cut out. Fuse to mitten front. Blanket-stitch around outside edge using three plies of floss. Make a contrasting cuff from fleece with blanket stitches around the bottom edge.
2. Assemble the mittens as described on *page 69*.

velvet embossed mittens

What you need
Velvet mitten fabric; lining fabric; fleece for cuff
Stamp for fabric embossing
Presscloth; iron
60 small rhinestones for mittens
32 large rhinestones for cuffs
Fabric/jewel glue

What to do
1. To emboss velvet, work on a hard, protected surface. Turn the stamp

upside down. Place the mitten front right side down on the stamp. Place slightly damp press cloth on fabric and press with medium hot iron (no steam) for 20 seconds. DO NOT slide the iron or rock it as this may distort the embossing. Test the fabric before beginning with mitten pieces.
2. Assemble the mittens as described on *page 69*. Glue on the rhinestone details.

ribbon-
trimmed
mittens

67

merry mittens

stem stitch

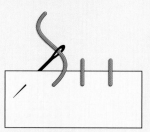

straight stitch

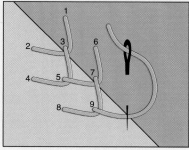

featherstitch

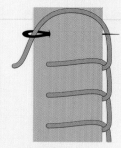

blanket stitch

snowman's nose—satin stitch

lazy daisy stitch

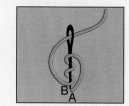

french knot

B A

mitten patterns

1 square = 1 inch

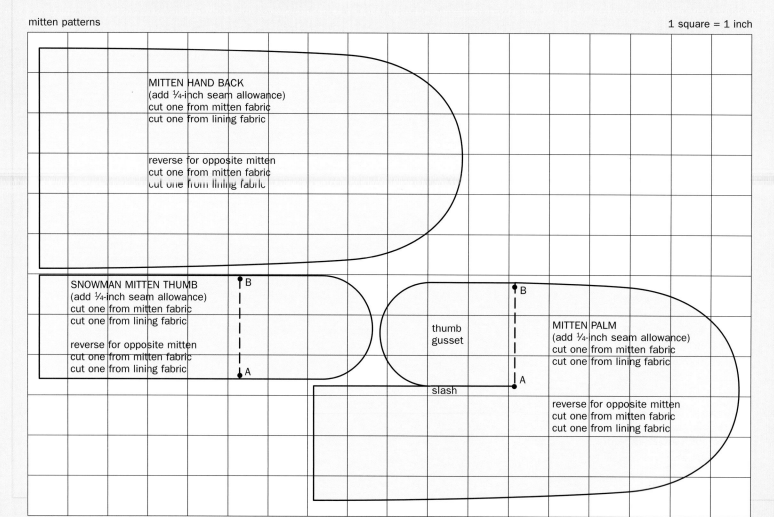

MITTEN HAND BACK
(add ¼-inch seam allowance)
cut one from mitten fabric
cut one from lining fabric

reverse for opposite mitten
cut one from mitten fabric
cut one from lining fabric

SNOWMAN MITTEN THUMB
(add ¼-inch seam allowance)
cut one from mitten fabric
cut one from lining fabric

reverse for opposite mitten
cut one from mitten fabric
cut one from lining fabric

B

A

B

A

thumb
gusset

MITTEN PALM
(add ¼-inch seam allowance)
cut one from mitten fabric
cut one from lining fabric

reverse for opposite mitten
cut one from mitten fabric
cut one from lining fabric

slash

snowman and snowflake mittens

What you need

Fusible web paper
*Black-and-white checked wool
 for mitten fabric; lining
 fabric; red velvet*
*5x5-inch piece of each of two
 different white fabrics*
2x3-inch piece of black fabric
2x3-inch piece of red fabric
*Black, brown, orange, red, and
 white cotton embroidery floss*
*2 red and six white heart
 buttons*
Two ⅜-inch buttons
6 white heart buttons

What to do

1. Trace the snowflake and
snowman patterns, *page 66*,
onto web paper. Fuse to
the corresponding fabrics
and then fuse to each
mitten front.

2. Add details using buttons
and embroidery stitches.
3. Assemble the mittens
as described *below*.

plaid taffeta with yo-yos mittens

What you need

*5 different color
 3¼-inch circles of satin*
5 sew-through buttons
*¾ yard of ⅜-inch-wide green
 grosgrain ribbon*

What to do

1. For yo-yo flowers
mittens, sew a running
stitch around the outside
edge of each satin circle.
Pull threads to gather
tightly. four yo-yos. Attach
three to one mitten with
buttons. Fold a 6-inch piece
of ribbon into a stem shape.
Add a ribbon-loop leaf

approximately 2½ inches
long. Topstitch in place.
2. For yo-yos-in-a-row
mittens, hand-stitch three
yo-yos to each mitten front.
Sew a button in the center
of each yo-yo.
3. Assemble the mittens
as described *below*.

What to do for all mittens

1. Enlarge and trace the
mitten pattern, *opposite*,
onto tracing paper and
cut out. Cut shapes
from mitten and
lining fabrics
(reversing the
shapes for the
opposite mitten).
2. Stitch mitten
seams with right
sides facing using a
¼-inch seam
allowance. Stitch the
thumb gusset around the
curved edge from A to B.

snowman
and snowflake
mittens

Stitch the inner seam of
thumb and palm, tapering
to a point at A. Cut the
elastic in half. Machine-
zigzag over the elastic
stretched on the wrong side
of the palm/thumb, 3
inches down from the top
edge. Trim the excess
elastic.
3. Stitch mitten palm to
back along side and finger
curve. Turn right side out.
4. Repeat for the lining,
leaving an opening for
turning in side seam.
5. Stitch ends of each cuff
together. Press seams open.
Fold cuff in half with wrong
sides facing and matching
raw edges.
6. Ease-stitch along the top
edge of the cuff and baste to
the mitten.
7. Slip mitten into lining,
matching side seams and
thumb. Stitch top edge.
Slip-stitch opening in lining
closed. Tuck the lining into
mitten and turn cuff down.

plaid taffeta with
yo-yos mittens

terrific tassels

As intricate as jewelry, these tiny tassels add a splash of color wherever they appear. Use these silky treasures on key chains, to spruce up a belt, or to tie to a gift.

school colors tassel

indian feather belt snap

tassel trio

sweetheart rose tassel

beads and
butterflies tassel
and striped tassel

71

terrific tassels

elegant beaded tassel

school colors tassel

What you need
#3 perle cotton in desired color
4½x5-inch piece of cardboard
Scissors
18mm lobster clasp
Wide-tooth comb; crewel needle
1½ yards of ¼-inch satin
* ribbon in desired color*
4mm and 6mm metallic beads
* in desired colors*

What to do
1. Wrap perle cotton 200 times around the 5-inch length of cardboard. Slide the threads together. Tie one end tightly using a 12-inch length of perle cotton. Using the same threads as used to tie the top, tie on the clasp. Lay these threads against the rest of the tassel threads. Cut at opposite end of the tassel. Remove from cardboard.
2. Comb through the threads until they lie flat. Using perle cotton, wrap the threads 20 times, ½ inch from the top. Knot and tuck the thread ends under using a crewel needle.
3. Cut four 12-inch lengths of ribbon. Thread a 12-inch length of ribbon on a crewel needle. Knot one end 1¼ inches from the end. Thread on three beads and run needle up under the wraps. Thread on a bead and bring the needle back down under the wraps. Thread on three more beads and knot end. Repeat three more times. Trim threads and ribbon ends.

indian feather belt snap

What you need
Orange #8 perle cotton
4½x5-inch piece of cardboard
Scissors; gold swivel clip
Wide-tooth comb
Crewel needle; 6 feather charms
Large seed beads in desired
* colors; silver bead wire*

What to do
1. Wrap perle cotton 200 times around the 5-inch length of cardboard. Slide the threads together. Cut one end. Remove from cardboard. Tie one end tightly using a 12-inch length of perle cotton.
2. Slip the tied end of the thread bundle through the base of the gold swivel. Pull

continued on page 74

Sources
- Purchase perle cotton and crewel needles in crafts and needlework stores. Substitute cotton embroidery floss for perle cotton if desired.
- Purchase jewelry findings and beads in crafts, fabric, and discount stores.

Sewing and finishing tips
- Experiment mixing various threads and yarns when making these tassels.
- If making several tassels, use a thin piece of plastic instead of cardboard to wrap threads around. Plastic will hold its shape longer.
- Keep bead groups separate by storing in containers, such as baby food jars or emptied pill bottles.

TO SELL IT
- Make matching sets to sell as pillow embellishments.

TO GIVE IT
- Loop a tassel around a perfume or bath oil bottle as an extra embellishment.

Cost to make project
$1 to $3 per tassel

Suggested selling price
$3 to $12 per tassel, depending on intricacy of detail and materials used

Time to make project
15 to 30 minutes

Timesaving tips
- Make several of the same-size tassels at a time using the same color of perle cotton.
- Have a sharp pair of scissors handy and tassel trimming will go much faster.
- Use a pincushion to hold needles when not in use.
- Place a pie tin on the work surface when making tassels. If a bead is dropped, it drops into the tin.

- Attach tassels to a variety of items to emphasize their versatility, such as on keys, a belt, door knob, wrapped gifts, ornaments, etc.

- Personalize a tassel by choosing special charms to attach to the wrap.

terrific tassels

the threads through until the center point is reached. Clip the tie at the end of the thread bundle. Holding the threads in the center, comb through the threads until they lie flat.

3. Using perle cotton, wrap the threads 20 times, 1/2 inch from the swivel. Tuck the thread ends under using a crewel needle.

4. Cut an 18-inch strand of perle cotton. Run the end through the feather charm, double the thread, leaving the feather at the center of the fold. Thread both ends onto a crewel needle. Thread on about 25 beads in desired pattern. Make five more strings of beads in this manner. To attach to the tassel, run the needle up through the bottom of the wraps, bring the needle through the swivel base, and insert the needle down through the wraps on the second side. (Do not pull too tightly; thread should lie neatly on top of the tassel threads.) Remove the end of the thread from the needle. Repeat to attach the five remaining groups of beads.

5. Thread 10 beads on the silver bead wire. Wrap around the tassel and twist the ends together. Repeat with another color. Trim wire ends and tuck into the tassel.

6. Trim the thread ends to the desired length.

tassel trio

What you need

#8 perle cotton in three desired colors
4 1/2x5-inch piece of cardboard
Scissors
Three large gold jewelry split rings
Wide-tooth comb
Crewel needle
Gold lanyard hook

What to do

1. Wrap one color perle cotton 50 times around the 4 1/2-inch length of cardboard. Slide the threads together. Cut one end. Remove from cardboard. Tightly tie one end of the bundle.

2. Slip the tied end of the thread bundle through the jewelry ring. Pull the threads through until the center point is reached. Clip the tie at the end of the thread bundle. Holding the threads in the center, comb through the threads until they lie flat.

3. Using perle cotton, wrap the threads 20 times 1/4 inch from the ring. Tuck the thread ends under using a crewel needle.

Trim the thread ends to the desired length.

4. Make two more tassels as described above. Slip the rings onto the lanyard hook. NOTE: For larger tassels, wrap perle cotton around the cardboard until the preferred thickness is achieved. If desired, sew a charm to the wrap as shown on *page 71* in the lower right-hand photograph.

sweetheart rose tassel

What you need

Hot pink #8 perle cotton
4 1/2x5-inch piece of cardboard
Scissors
Gold swivel clip
Wide-tooth comb
Crewel needle
Gold bead wire
4mm gold beads
Four 1-inch hot pink silk roses with leaves

What to do

1. Wrap perle cotton 200 times around the 5-inch length of cardboard. Slide the threads together. Cut one end. Remove from

cardboard. Tightly tie one end of the bundle.

2. Slip the tied end of the thread bundle through the base of the gold swivel. Pull the threads through until the center point is reached. Clip the tie at the end of the thread bundle. Holding the threads in the center, comb through the threads until they lie flat.

3. Using perle cotton, wrap the threads 20 times, 1/2 inch from the swivel. Tuck the thread ends under using a crewel needle.

4. Thread the crewel needle with bead wire. Run needle under the wraps from the bottom to the top. Wrap the beads around the tassel, covering the wrap area. Wrap both ends of wire together. Thread wire back onto crewel needle and bring down through the wrap area. Trim the end.

5. Thread needle with perle cotton and knot ends. Push needle down through wrap area, coming out below beading. Sew on satin rose. Push needle through the same spot and bring out at the top of the wrap. Continue sewing on roses in this manner. When completed, bring needle up through the top, reinsert and push down through the center of the tassel. Remove needle.

6. Trim the thread ends to the desired length.

beads and butterflies tassel

What you need

Purple #8 perle cotton
4½x5-inch piece of cardboard
12mm lobster clasp
Scissors
Wide-tooth comb
Crewel needle
4 butterfly charms
Blue seed beads
Silver beading wire

What to do

1. Wrap perle cotton 200 times around the 5-inch length of cardboard. Slide the threads together. Tie one end tightly using a 12-inch length of perle cotton. Using the same threads as used to tie the tassel top, tie on the lobster clasp. Lay these threads against the rest of the tassel threads. Cut threads at opposite end of the tassel. Remove from cardboard.
2. Comb through the threads until they lie flat. Using perle cotton, wrap the threads twenty times, ½ inch from the top. Knot and tuck the thread ends under using a crewel needle.
3. Loosely sew butterfly charms to the bottom of the wrapped area.

4. Thread beads onto wire to wind around wrapped area three times. Twist ends together, trim wire ends, and tuck into tassel.
5. Trim tassel threads to desired length.

striped tassel

What you need

#8 perle cotton in two desired colors
4½x5-inch piece of cardboard
Scissors
Large gold jewelry split ring
Wide-tooth comb; crewel needle
½-inch plastic ring

What to do

1. Wrap one color perle cotton 50 times around the 4½-inch length of cardboard. Slide the threads together. Using a doubled length of perle cotton, tie one end. Cut opposite end.
2. Thread the needle with the ends of the perle cotton ties. Sew around split ring and tie thread until secure. Bring ends through center of tassel. Remove needle.
3. Comb through the threads until they lie flat.

Using perle cotton, wrap the threads 20 times. ½ inch from the ring. Tuck the thread ends under using a crewel needle. Trim thread ends to desired length.
4. Wrap the same color of perle cotton 24 times around the 4½-inch length of cardboard. Clip at the bottom. Push loop end of perle cotton bundle through the plastic ring. Pull the tails through the loops. Continue covering the plastic ring, alternating colors, until eight groupings of threads are attached. Slip the ring over the tassel top. Tack the ring in place if needed.
5. Trim tassel ends even at desired length.

elegant beaded tassel

What you need

Cream #8 perle cotton
4½x5-inch piece of cardboard
Silver bead cap; lanyard hook
Crewel needle; scissors
Wide-tooth comb
Silver thread
4mm silver beads

What to do

1. Wrap perle cotton 200 times around the 4½-inch length of cardboard. Slide the threads together. Tie one end tightly using a doubled 12-inch length of perle cotton. Slip the bead cap over the tied threads. Tie on the lanyard hook. Thread ends on crewel needle and draw down through the hole in the bead cap. Cut the threads at the opposite end of the tassel. Remove the perle cotton threads from the cardboard.
2. Comb through the threads until they lie flat. Using silver thread, wrap the threads (not too tightly) 16 times, ½ inch from the top. Knot the thread and tuck the ends under using a crewel needle.
3. Thread a double strand of silver thread in needle and knot ends. Thread on four silver beads. Push needle up under the silver wraps, thread on bead, and push back down under the wraps. Thread on four beads and knot the end. Repeat three times.
4. Stitch a ring of beads around the bottom of the wrap.
5. Trim the tassel threads to the desired length.

clever crocheted mats
and napkin rings

Made from three plies of yarn, these place mats and napkin rings will protect tabletops from scratches while adding a touch of pizzazz.

place mat

What you need
*1½ oz./42.5g. cotton 4-ply worsted-weight yarn—2 skeins of solid color, 3 skeins of multicolored yarn
Crochet hook size J
3 yards of 2¼-inch-wide ribbon*

What to do
1. Holding one strand of each yarn color together, chain 27. Sc in 2nd ch from hook, draw up a lp in same ch as first sc, draw up a lp in next ch, yo and draw through 3 lps on hook. * Draw up a lp in same ch as last st, draw up a lp in next ch, yo and draw through all 3 lps on hook; rep from * across – 26 sts; turn.
2. Ch 1, sc in first st, draw up a lp in same st as first sc, draw up a lp in next sc, yo and draw through 3 lps on hook. * Draw up a lp in same st as last st, draw up a lp in next st, yo and draw through all 3 lps on hook; rep from * across; turn. Rep this row for 38 times more. Fasten off.

3. Join one strand of multicolored yarn with a sl st in right corner. In same sp as join, (sc, hdc, dc, hdc, sc – scallop made). Working along one short edge first, * sk next st, make a scallop in the next st; rep from * across to corner. For long edge, * sk 1 row, make a scallop in side of next row; rep from * to corner. Work rem sides as established. At end, join with a sl st in first sc and fasten off.
4. Beginning at top center, weave ribbon under and over every two crochet stitches one row in from edge. Tie ends into a bow.

napkin ring

What you need
*1 skein #3 perle cotton
1½-inch-diameter plastic ring
Size 3 steel crochet hook*

What to do
1. Join cotton to ring with a sl st. Ch 1, work 32 sc around the ring. * Ch 3, sk 1 sc, sc in next sc; rep from * around. In each ch-3 sp work (sc, hdc, dc, hdc, sc). At end, join with sl st in first sc and fasten off.

Sources
- Purchase yarn in crafts, discount, and fabric stores as well as in knitting and crochet shops.
- Purchase plastic rings near the drapery accessories in discount, fabric and home decor stores.

Crochet abbreviations
*ch—chain
dc—double crochet
hdc—half double crochet
lp(s)—loop(s)
rep—repeat
sc—single crochet
sk—skip
sl st—slip stitch
sp—space
st(s)—stitch(es)
yo—yarn over*

Sewing and finishing tips
- Scraps of yarns can be combined to make a multicolored mat.

Cost to make project
$4 for a mat and napkin set

Suggested selling price
$15 for a set

Time to make project
2 hours

Timesaving tip
- Once you've made a mat or two, this project is a great in-the-car project.

TO SELL IT
- Make a display on a portable serving tray, complete with dishes, silverware, and a flower.
- Provide washing instructions for the mat.
- Make several sets in the same color scheme for large families or for entertaining purposes.

TO GIVE IT
- To mail these sets, roll the mats around a paper tube, wrap, tie with a ribbon bow, and place into a larger mailing tube.
- For a special in-bed breakfast, place a mat atop a lap tray, place a cloth napkin into the ring and serve a delicious recipe.

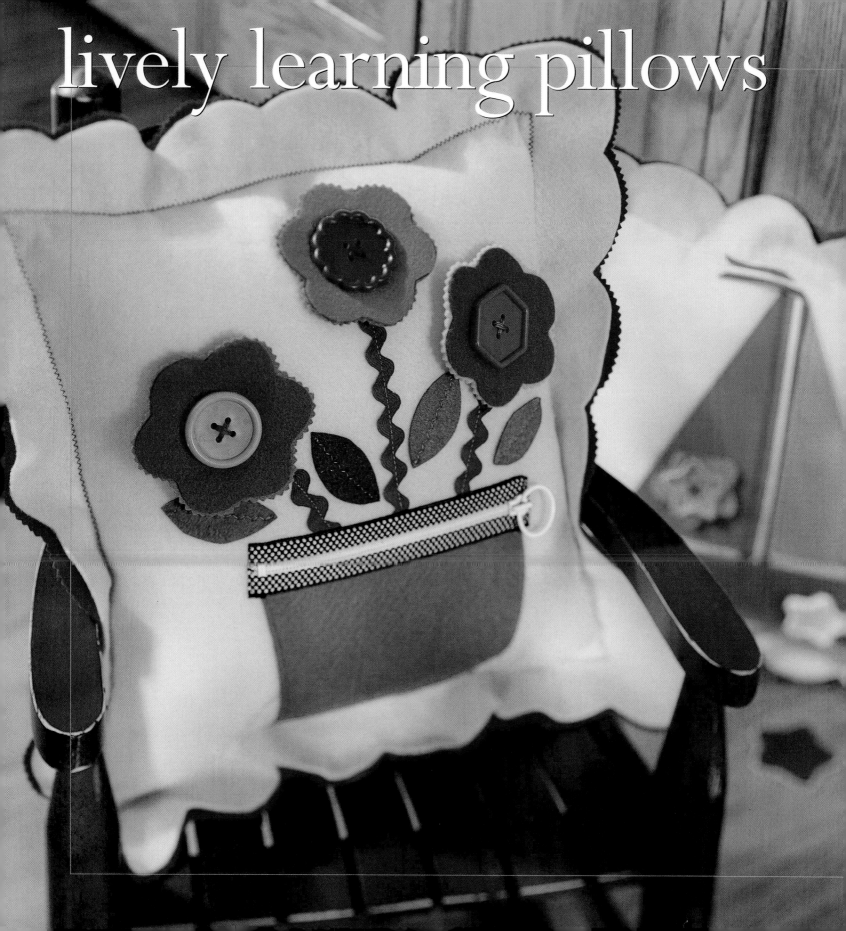

Fun and educational, these bright pillows will delight toddlers as they exclaim, "I did it myself!" The simple shapes help teach primary colors as well as how to button and zip.

What you need for all pillows
Fusible web paper
Scissors
Two 15x15-inch squares of felt in desired colors
Pinking sheers
Polyester pillow stuffing

What you need for flowerpot pillow
8x8-inch piece of felt for pot
5x10-inch pieces of felt in 3 colors for flowers
3 large buttons
7-inch-long novelty zipper
Green felt scraps for leaves
Ribbon, rickrack, or other trim for stems

What you need for sailboat pillow
4x12-inch piece of felt for boat
Two 5x10-inch pieces of felt in different colors for sails
Scrap of ribbon for flag
12-inch-long novelty zipper
Two star buttons

What to do for both pillows
1. Trace the desired pattern pieces from *pages 80–83* onto fusible web paper. Fuse pieces to desired felts and cut out. Using the diagram on *page 80* as a guide, cut scallops around the edges of the 15x15-inch pillow back using pinking sheers. Make the front piece slightly smaller and cut scallops in the front piece using scissors. Arrange the felt shapes on the pillow front, 2 inches from the scalloped edge. Fuse in place.
2. Machine-stitch around outside edges using matching thread. Topstitch zippers as shown in the photograph, *opposite and right.*
3. For flower pillow, stitch the stems and ribbon leaves to the pillow. Cut out flowers using pinking sheers and regular scissors, and fuse together. Sew buttons onto pillow. Make a slit in flowers for buttonhole.
4. For boat pillow, cut out stars using pinking sheers and regular scissors, and fuse together. Sew buttons onto pillows. Make a slit in stars for buttonhole. Sew ribbon to boat for mast and flag.
5. For both pillows, layer front and back, wrong sides facing. Topstitch through layers, leaving an opening at the bottom. Add stuffing. Stitch opening closed.

Sources
- Purchase felt as precut rectangles or by the yard. For the front and back pillow pieces you will need to buy it by the yard in fabric and discount stores.
- Purchase polyester stuffing (fiberfill) in fabric, crafts, and discount stores.

Sewing and finishing tip
- Using a pinking sheer to cut felt adds a nice finishing touch. Look at the photo, *left,* to see where we used these zig-zag cuts.

TO SELL IT
- Use the flower or star pattern to cut price tags from coordinating paper.
- Have a pillow of each design labeled, "Try Me." Any children that stop at your booth, can practice their skills.

TO GIVE IT
- To further help teach a child, provide additional felt flowers or stars in various colors to aid the child in learning colors.

Cost to make project
$4

Suggested selling price
$17.50 for one

Time to make project
2 hours

Timesaving tip
- Cut several fabric pieces at once and assemble 6 or 10 in stages.

- Include safety instructions with pillows. It is not for children under two and should not be used for sleeping.
- Carefully wrap each pillow in white tissue paper when selling to a customer.

- When you give a child one of these pillows, turn it into a game. See if she can point to shapes, such as circles, stars, and triangles.

lively
learning
pillows

flower pillow placement diagram

flower pillow
small flower pattern

flower pillow
large flower pattern

flower pillow
leaf patterns

flower pillow
flowerpot pattern

lively learning pillows

sailboat pillow placement diagram

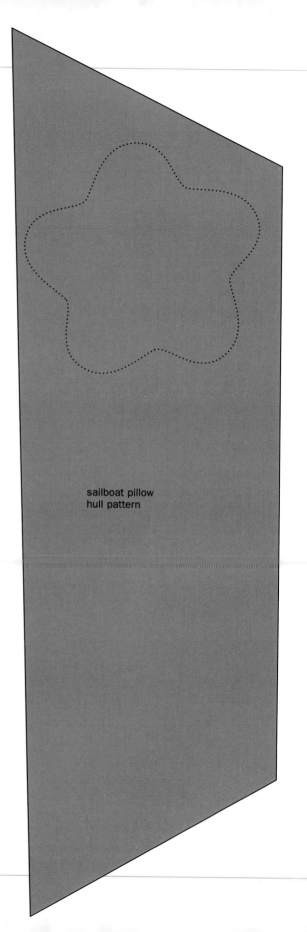

sailboat pillow
hull pattern

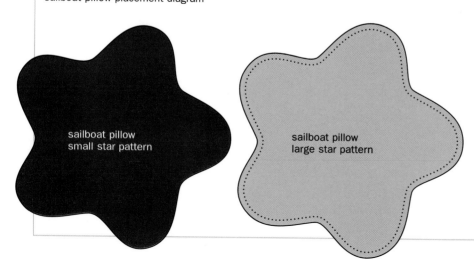

sailboat pillow
small star pattern

sailboat pillow
large star pattern

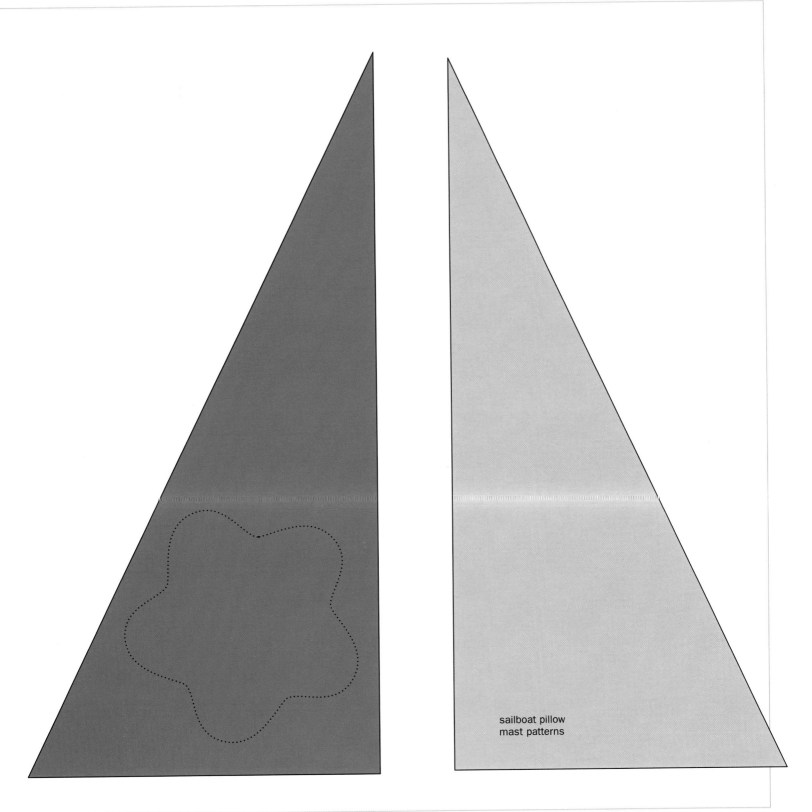

sailboat pillow
mast patterns

velvet fruit pincushions

These elegant fruits stand tall on glistening glass bases. Pretty enough to adorn a mantel or centerpiece, these velvet versions do double duty as pincushions.

apple pincushion

What you need

Tracing paper and pencil
Large scraps of velvet (regular or crushed) in apple colors
Fiberfill
Soap-filled scouring pad
Pipe cleaner
Carpet thread and long doll needle
Thick white crafts glue
Short glass candlesticks
Waxed cord
Braid or other desired trim
Floral tape in green and brown
Artificial velvet leaves
Glitter paint, optional
Sequins and seed beads

What to do

1. Trace the apple pattern from *page 86*. Cut four of the sections for each apple from velvet. Follow the arrow on the pattern for the direction of the grain.
2. With right sides facing, baste two sections together along one side, stopping at the dot on the top of each section. Machine-stitch using a ¼-inch seam. Add the next section, baste, and stitch. Stitch the edge of the last section to the edge of the first section and turn the apple right side out through the bottom opening.
3. Use fiberfill to stuff the top and outside edges of the apple. Push scouring pad into the center of the apple and continue to stuff with fiberfill until apple is firmly stuffed. The scouring pad will help keep pins and needles sharp.
4. For the stem, cut the pipe cleaner into thirds. Fold one third in half and twist both sides of the pipe cleaner together. Thread the doll needle with a long doubled length of carpet thread. Knot the end of the thread and loop the needle and thread through the folded end of the twisted stem. Insert needle down through the center top of the apple, pushing the needle through fiberfill and scouring pad until it comes out the bottom of the fruit. Cut the needle from the thread. Tie two ends of the thread tightly into a knot, pulling the stem snug into the top of the apple and causing a slight indentation. Cut off any excess thread.

continued on page 86

Sources
- Purchase velvet in discount, crafts, and fabric stores. Check the fabrics on bolts as well as velvets found with the upholstery fabrics.
- Look for candlesticks in discount, crafts, home decor, and candle stores as well as in flea markets and garage sales.

Sewing and finishing tips
- Once you've mastered these, try making your own patterns for oranges, plums, and peaches.
- For more detail, decorate the candlestick with paint.

- If your fabric tends to fray, check for products in the fabric store that will stop the process.

Cost to make project
$3

Suggested selling price
$12

Time to make project
2 hours

Timesaving tips
- Layer fabrics to cut several pieces at once.
- Keep embellishments to a minimum.

TO SELL IT

- Place a sign by the pincushions that reads, "Practical and Pretty."
- Suggest other uses such as mantel decorations or centerpieces—displaying with a candle arrangement.
- To make an interesting display, intermix the pincushions with baskets of fresh fruit.
- Place large needles and pins in a few of the display pincushions, but keep out of the reach of children to avoid injury.

TO GIVE IT

- Place a fruit pincushion in the center of a basket and fill in with the real thing.
- Wrap the pincushion with fruit-inspired paper, adding miniature artificial fruit to the center of the bow.

velvet fruit pincushions

apple pincushion pattern
(cut four)

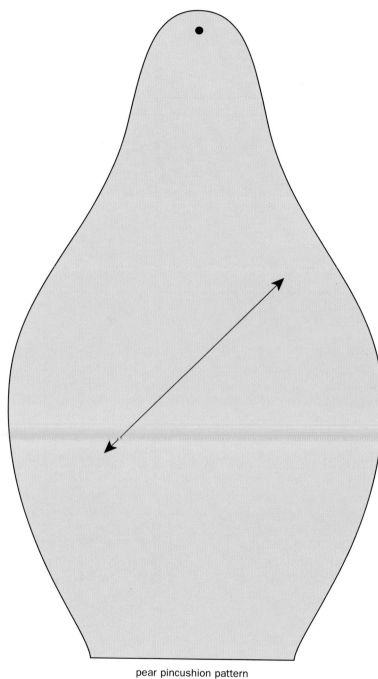

pear pincushion pattern
(cut four)

5. Apply glue around the upper portion (neck) of the candlestick. Use your finger to make an indentation in the fiberfill along the bottom edge of the apple. Slip the apple over the top of candlestick, pulling the bottom edges of fabric down over the upper portion of the candlestick. Center the apple and hold the edges securely with fingers around the candlestick. Wrap a long piece of waxed cord three to four times around the fabric and candlestick. Secure with a double knot and cut off the excess cord.
6. Glue braid or other desired trim over the wrapped fabric and cording.
7. Wrap the stem with floral tape. Secure a leaf near the stem with glue or a pin. Leaves can be decorated with beads or glitter paint if desired.
8. Add sequins and seed beads to the apple. Slip colorful beads on a long corsage pin to stick in the pincushion if desired.

pear pincushion

What you need
Tracing paper and pencil
Large scraps of velvet (regular or crushed) in pear colors
Fiberfill
Soap-filled scouring pad
Pipe cleaner
Carpet thread and long doll needle
Thick white crafts glue
Short glass candlesticks
Waxed cord
Trims such as ribbon, cording, and braid
Floral tape in green and brown
Artificial velvet leaves
Glitter paint, optional
Beads on a string

What to do
1. Trace the pear pattern, opposite. Cut four of the sections for each pear from velvet. Follow the arrow on the pattern for the direction of the grain.
2. With right sides facing, baste two sections together along one side, stopping at the dot on the top of each section. Machine-stitch using a ¼-inch seam. Add the next section, baste, and stitch. Stitch the edge of the last section to the edge of the first section and turn the pear right side out through bottom opening.

3. Use fiberfill to stuff the top and outside edges of the pear. Push scouring pad into the center of the pear and continue to stuff with fiberfill until fruit is firmly stuffed. (The scouring pad will help keep pins and needles sharp.)
4. For the stem, cut the pipe cleaner into thirds. Fold one third in half and twist both sides of the pipe cleaner together. Thread the doll needle with a long doubled length of carpet thread. Knot the end of the thread and loop the needle and thread through the folded end of the twisted stem. Insert needle down through the center top of the pear, pushing the needle through fiberfill and scouring pad until it comes out the bottom of the pear. Cut the needle from the thread. Tie two ends of the thread tightly into a knot, pulling the stem snug into the top of the pear and causing a slight indentation. Cut off any excess thread.

5. Apply glue around the upper portion (neck) of the candlestick. Use your finger to make an indentation in the fiberfill along the bottom edge of the pear. Slip the fruit over the top of candlestick, pulling the bottom edges of fabric down over the upper portion of the candlestick. Center the fruit and hold the edges securely with fingers around the candlestick. Wrap a long piece of waxed cord three to four times around the fabric and candlestick. Secure with a double knot. Cut off excess cord.
6. Glue braid or other desired trim over the wrapped fabric and cording.
7. Wrap the stem with floral tape. Secure a leaf near the stem with glue or a pin. Leaves can be decorated with beads or glitter paint if desired.
8. Add strands of beads by tacking to the pear near the stem. Slip colorful beads on a long corsage pin to stick in the pincushion if desired.

adorable doll duo

Just the right size for children's hands, these sweet dolls have charming details. Stitch them from muslin or Jobelan then add either cross-stitched accents or drawn-on faces.

What you need for both dolls

Tracing paper; pencil; scissors
Black, blue, red, and brown permanent markers
Cotton embroidery floss in colors listed in key on page 90
Two additional skeins of deep mahogany (DMC 300) embroidery floss
Embroidery hoop; needle
Threads to match fabrics
$3^{1}/_{4}$-inch-wide piece of cardboard
Polyester fiberfill
Cosmetic blush and small brush
$^{1}/_{8}$-inch-wide elastic
Four $^{1}/_{4}$-inch-diameter snaps

What you need for the boy

*Two 8x10-inch pieces of 28-count ivory Jobelan fabric **or** muslin for body*
Two 5x6-inch pieces of plaid fabric for vest
5x$8^{1}/_{2}$-inch piece of cotton fabric for vest lining
$5^{1}/_{2}$x9-inch piece of red fabric for shirt
Two $4^{1}/_{4}$x3-inch pieces of dark green fabric for pants

What you need for the girl

*Two 8x10-inch pieces of 28-count ivory Jobelan fabric **or** muslin for body*
4x$9^{1}/_{4}$-inch piece of plaid fabric for apron
$1^{7}/_{8}$x$2^{1}/_{2}$-inch piece of plaid fabric for apron bib
5x9-inch piece of red fabric for dress
$1^{7}/_{8}$x$2^{1}/_{2}$-inch piece of tan fabric for apron bib lining
1x$26^{1}/_{2}$-inch piece of dark blue fabric for apron details

What to do for both dolls

1. Trace body and clothing patterns, *page 90*, onto tracing paper and cut out pattern pieces.
2. For clothing, use patterns to cut pieces from designated fabrics. Seams will be sewn with the right sides facing.
3. For body, trace around pattern in the center of one Jobelan *or* muslin fabric piece. Measure and mark tops of shoes. DO NOT cut out. If stitching the face details on Jobelan fabric, center nose on body front face, leaving 30 threads

continued on page 91

Sources

- Purchase embroidery floss and cross-stitch fabrics, such as Jobelan, in stitchery shops. The cross-stitched version of this project is stitched over two threads of 28-count Jobelan. Since there are no fractional stitches, a 14-count fabric could be substituted. If a 14-count fabric is used, work stitches over one square of fabric.

Sewing and finishing tips

- For the girl, add matching bows to her hair using narrow satin ribbon.
- Use a comb to straighten the floss hair on the dolls.

Cost to make project

$10 for the set

Suggested selling price

$15 for one, $26 for both

Time to make project

1½ hours

Timesaving tips

- Replace cross-stitched facial features with permanent marker (both patterns are given on page 90).
- Layer fabric and cut two or three pattern pieces at once using sharp scissors.
- Make and assemble the dolls in stages to make the process efficient.

TO SELL IT

- Make dolls with various colors of hair and eyes.
- Sell the duo as a set, with a change of clothing in a different color.
- At Christmas sales, display the dolls peeking out from miniature stockings.
- Make the clothing even fancier by adding tiny buttons, beads, or premade satin flowers.

TO GIVE IT

- Personalize the dolls for children by using floss colors that resemble their hair colors.

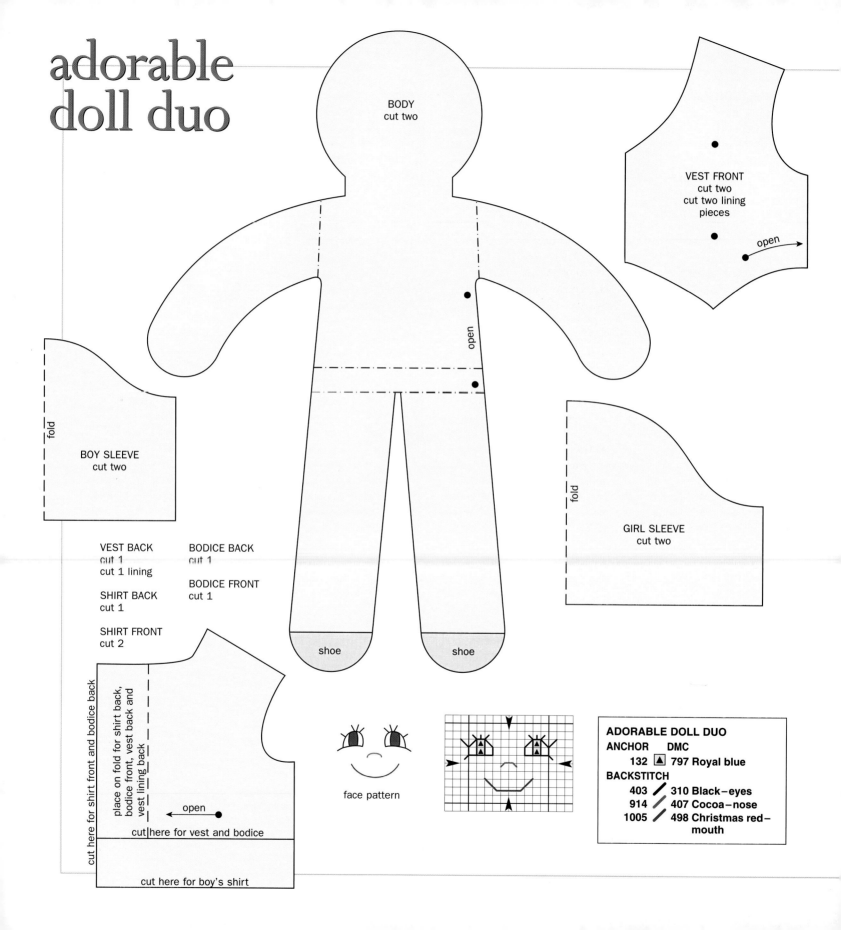

adorable doll duo

BODY
cut two

VEST FRONT
cut two
cut two lining
pieces

open

open

BOY SLEEVE
cut two

fold

GIRL SLEEVE
cut two

fold

VEST BACK
cut 1
cut 1 lining

BODICE BACK
cut 1

SHIRT BACK
cut 1

BODICE FRONT
cut 1

SHIRT FRONT
cut 2

shoe

shoe

cut here for shirt front and bodice back

place on fold for shirt back, bodice front, vest back and vest lining back

open

cut here for vest and bodice

cut here for boy's shirt

face pattern

ADORABLE DOLL DUO

ANCHOR		DMC	
132	▲	797	Royal blue

BACKSTITCH

403	╱	310	Black—eyes
914	╱	407	Cocoa—nose
1005	╱	498	Christmas red—mouth

between the top of nose and top of head. Stitch the face according to the chart, *opposite*. Use two plies of floss to work cross-stitches over two threads of fabric. Work backstitches and straight stitches using one ply over two threads of fabric.

4. Layer the two pieces of Jobelan *or* muslin fabrics with the traced pattern up. Pin the two fabric pieces together. Using very small machine stitches, stitch around traced line, leaving open between dots. (NOTE: The body pieces are actual size.) Restitch inner legs and inside curves. Trim the body shape $\frac{1}{4}$ inch from the stitching, leaving a wider seam allowance at the opening. Carefully clip the curves and turn.

5. Using a black permanent marker, color in shoe area. If drawing the face on muslin, use the pattern *opposite* as a guide. Draw in the details with permanent marker.

6. Stuff limbs, leaving top $\frac{3}{4}$ inch of legs and top $\frac{1}{2}$ inch of arms unstuffed. Stitch across top of legs and shoulder areas as indicated by dotted lines (so legs and arms will move). Stuff head and body, leaving $\frac{1}{2}$ inch of body bottom unstuffed; sew opening closed. Stitch body bottom along dotted lines.

7. For boy's hair, wrap deep mahogany floss 20 times around $3\frac{1}{4}$-inch cardboard. Slide loops off card and spread center of wrapped floss to measure 1 inch.

Machine-stitch across center to make part. Hand-stitch part to head top using floss. Pull loops down; hand-stitch to nape of neck. Spread loops as necessary to cover back of head.

8. For bangs, use floss from same skein as boy's hair. Wrap floss five times around three fingers, cut off, tie around center, and cut loops. Use point of pin to separate strands. Hand-stitch bangs to front part; trim to shape.

9. For girl's hair, spread center of full skein of deep mahogany floss to measure $1\frac{1}{2}$ inches. Stitch across center to make part. Hand-stitch part to head top using floss. Gather loops at each side below ear level; tie with scrap of floss for pigtails. Make bangs as for boy.

10. Make rosy cheeks using blush and small brush.

11. For boy's shirt, turn under $\frac{1}{4}$ inch twice along center front edges to hem; stitch. Using a $\frac{1}{4}$-inch seam, sew fronts to back at shoulders. Stitch around neck $\frac{1}{4}$ inch from edge. Clip to stitching, press under along seamline, and edge-stitch. Gather sleeve tops to fit armholes; stitch. Turn under $\frac{1}{4}$ inch twice along sleeve bottoms to hem; stitch. Sew sleeve/side seams. Hem shirt bottom as for sleeves. Sew two snaps to center front.

12. For boy's pants, turn up $\frac{1}{4}$ inch twice along one short edge of each $4\frac{1}{4}$x3-inch pant piece. Stitch to hem. Lay pant pieces together right

sides facing. Mark point $1\frac{3}{4}$ inches below unhemmed top edges on one side. Sew pieces together from top edge to mark using $\frac{1}{4}$-inch seam allowance to make center front seam. Open piece out. Press the top raw edge as for hem. Lay elastic within fold and sew casing closed. Secure one elastic end, pull elastic to fit waist, and secure opposite end. Sew the center back seam as for center front seam. Sew the leg inseams.

13. For boy's vest, sew fronts to back at side seams. Repeat for lining. Sew vest to lining, leaving open between dots. Clip curves and trim seams, leaving wider seam allowance at opening. Turn to right side, press, and sew opening closed. Hand-sew shoulder seams.

14. For girl's dress bodice, turn under $\frac{1}{4}$ inch twice along center back edges to hem; stitch. Sew fronts to back at shoulders. Finish neck and sew in sleeves as for shirt. Press sleeve bottoms as for hem. Lay elastic within fold and sew casing closed. On each sleeve, secure one end of elastic, pull elastic to fit arm, and secure opposite end. Sew sleeve/side seams.

15. To finish dress, hem one long edge of $3\frac{3}{4}$x3-inch skirt strip in same manner as other hems. Press under $\frac{1}{4}$ inch on short ends. Gather a long (top) edge to fit bodice bottom edge; stitch. Beginning at hem, sew

center back seam. Sew snaps to bodice back.

16. For pinafore, press 1x26$\frac{1}{2}$-inch waistband and strap piece in half lengthwise. Press both long raw edges under to meet first fold. Cut the 26$\frac{1}{2}$-inch piece into a 20-inch-long waistband and two 3$\frac{1}{4}$-inch-long straps. Hem pinafore 3-inch-length skirt sides and bottom in same manner as other hems. Gather top edge to measure 3$\frac{1}{4}$ inches. Center gathered top along waistband and encase edge in fold, allowing waistband ends to extend for ties. Topstitch along waistband, securing skirt. Knot ends of ties.

17. Sew bib to lining, folding bib piece in half to sew ends, leaving bottom open. Turn, press, and sew opening closed. Position bib bottom edge, centered, behind waistband. Stitch bib to skirt along previous topstitching.

18. Sew folded strap edges together. Turn ends under and hand-stitch each to wrong side of bib top. Fit straps over shoulders and tuck under waistband. Sew straps in place along previous waistband stitching.

19. Press all pieces lightly and dress the dolls.

for-all-seasons place cards

Help someone turn an ordinary dinner into a special gathering with these quick-stitch cards. Group them in matching sets to sell as place cards or sell one of each to use as gift tags.

Sources
- Purchase perforated paper and embroidery floss in crafts, discount, and stitchery stores.
- Purchase paper labels in discount and office supply stores.

Sewing and finishing tips
- To make gift tags using the same techniques, cut the perforated paper on the fold and adjust the backstitched border.
- To turn these paper place cards into permanent ornaments for a miniature tree, stitch on fabric and back with felt.

Cost to make project
25¢ per place card

Suggested selling price
$1.50 per place card or $10 per set

Time to make project
20 minutes per card

Timesaving tips
- Instead of stitching it, draw in the border using permanent marker.
- Precut labels, but let customer affix to the place cards.
- Separate floss into two-ply sections before beginning to stitch.
- Use a crafts knife and ruler to cut the perforated paper into rectangles.

What you need
2⅝x4¾-inch pieces of 14-count white perforated paper
Cotton embroidery thread as listed in key on page 94
Tapestry needle
Scissors
1x2¾-inch all-purpose white paper label with adhesive on one side
Ruler
Pencil

What to do
1. Fold the perforated paper in half so it measures 2⅝x2⅜ inches with the fold at the top.
2. Stitching through one layer of paper only, stitch the black border using one ply of embroidery floss and backstitches. This border is two holes in from all edges.
3. Following the chart and color key, *pages 94–95*, cross-stitch the chosen design using two plies of embroidery floss.

4. After all stitching is completed, use one ply of black embroidery floss and backstitches to outline all areas indicated on the chart. To make the star on the flag, use two plies of white embroidery floss. Each line of the star is a long stitch. To make dots on the strawberry and eyes on the turkey, use one ply of black embroidery floss and French knots. For the dots on the Easter egg, use one ply of embroidery floss as noted in color key, and French knots.
5. Clip extra threads on back of the stitched piece.
6. For the name placement on each place card, cut a paper label to measure 1¾x1 inch. Remove the paper backing from label. Center the label at the bottom of the place card front between the cross-stitched design and the bottom border, centered left to right. Push the label firmly in place.

TO SELL IT
- Display a place card at a creative table setting.
- Bundle several of the same motifs together to encourage multiple sales.

TO GIVE IT
- If you know someone has a special upcoming party, stitch several of the same seasonal motifs as a hostess gift.
- Make gift tags for major holidays and give with wrapping papers and ribbons.

for-all-seasons place cards

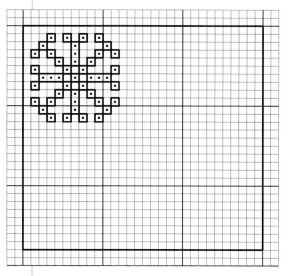

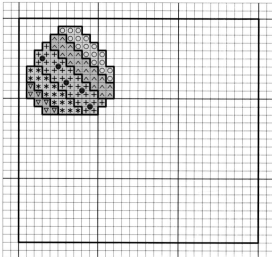

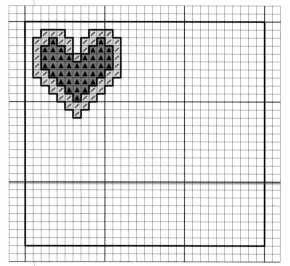

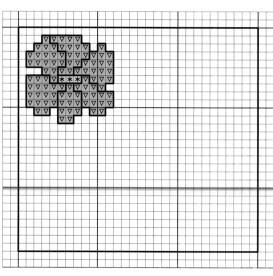

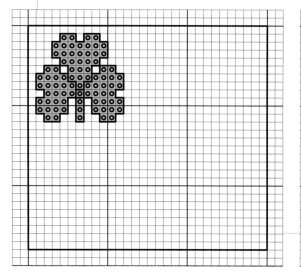

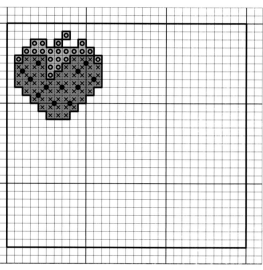

FOR-ALL-SEASONS PLACE CARDS

ANCHOR		DMC
002	·	000 White
403	■	310 Black
9046	✕	321 True Christmas red
310	⊞	434 Chestnut
1045	−	436 Dark tan
1005	▲	498 Dark Christmas red
063	∧	602 Cranberry
332	⊠	608 Orange
228	⊙	700 Christmas green
238	+	703 Chartreuse
1021	╱	761 Light salmon
176	▽	793 Cornflower blue
133	✤	796 Royal blue
1014	⋈	919 Red-copper
340	◆	920 Medium copper
338	⊕	921 True copper
1003	‖	922 Light copper
298	✳	972 Canary
167	◎	3766 Peacock blue

BACKSTITCH

403	╱	310 Black

FRENCH KNOT

403	●	310 Black
1005	●	498 Dark Christmas red

STAR STITCH

002	✳	000 White

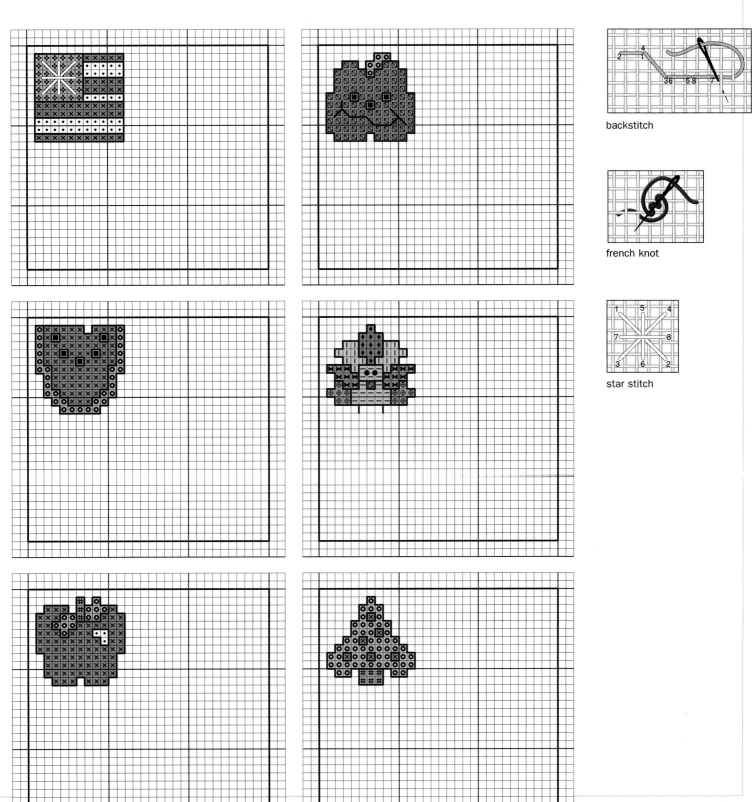

backstitch

french knot

star stitch

MAKE IT
WITH
WOOD

Made from wood, each of the projects in this chapter

has simple cuts with clever and sure-to-sell color combinations.

Whether you're new to woodworking or find a

workbench to be your second home, you'll be churning out

these projects by the dozens——ready for gift-giving

and crafts shows year-round.

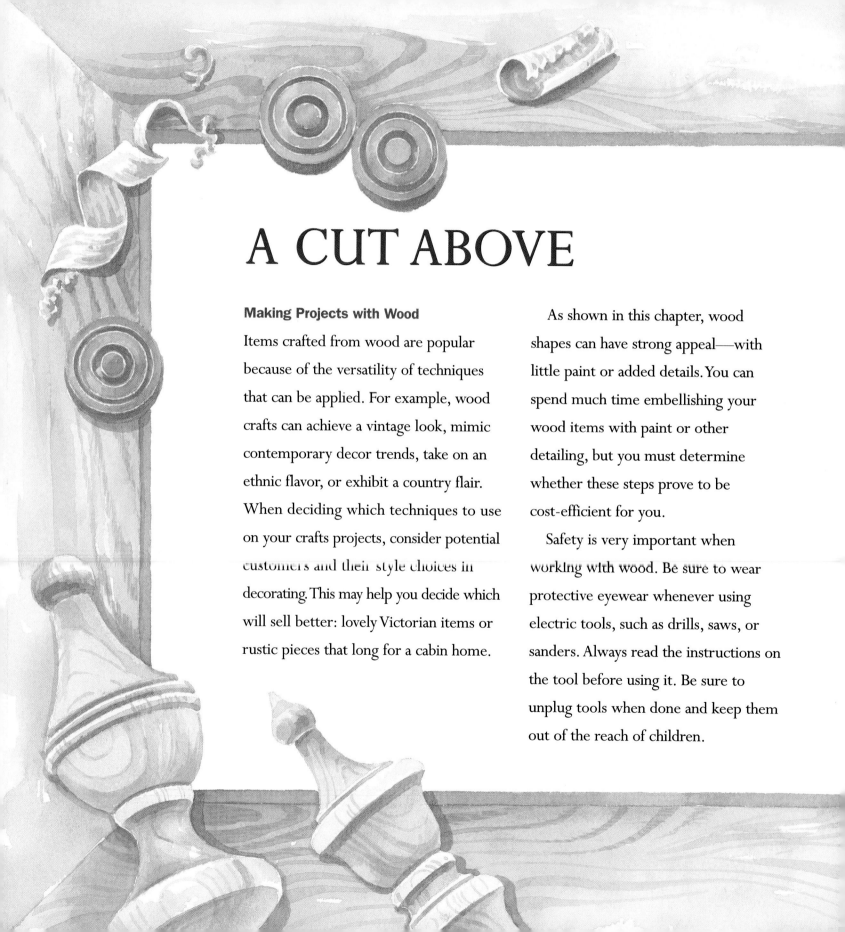

A CUT ABOVE

Making Projects with Wood

Items crafted from wood are popular because of the versatility of techniques that can be applied. For example, wood crafts can achieve a vintage look, mimic contemporary decor trends, take on an ethnic flavor, or exhibit a country flair. When deciding which techniques to use on your crafts projects, consider potential customers and their style choices in decorating. This may help you decide which will sell better: lovely Victorian items or rustic pieces that long for a cabin home.

As shown in this chapter, wood shapes can have strong appeal—with little paint or added details. You can spend much time embellishing your wood items with paint or other detailing, but you must determine whether these steps prove to be cost-efficient for you.

Safety is very important when working with wood. Be sure to wear protective eyewear whenever using electric tools, such as drills, saws, or sanders. Always read the instructions on the tool before using it. Be sure to unplug tools when done and keep them out of the reach of children.

Selling Wood Items

The way you display your wood projects may help lure customers to your booth or table. If the pieces have country appeal, you may want to use vintage step stools, watering cans, or wagons as part of your display. Another clever way to exhibit wood crafts is to prop them on old crates, trunks, hatboxes, furniture, or books. Think up ways to display your creations at different heights and to bring interest to your booth.

Because people decorate using many color schemes, vary color choices for your projects. Use vivid primary colors, pastels, or country hues. A simple change in color may make a project appeal to a specific customer.

For projects that have a function, such as the coasters on *pages 108–113*, display them in use. For example, place a pair of coasters on a game table with a deck of cards or game pieces. For wood creations that have multiple uses, indicate this on individual tags that attach to projects or on a very visible sign.

If there are special care instructions for your projects, include them with each purchase. This information will be an added benefit to your customers, and it's also a good place to put your name and address to aid in future sales. You also may want to include such information as how to place special orders, other crafts shows where you will be exhibiting, e-mail or website addresses, and other types of crafting projects you offer for sale.

stand-up stars

The shape of a star, with its jetting points, always catches the eye. This collection of wood stars is no exception. Painted in antique toy colors, some stars in the collection are trimmed with vintage buttons, torn-fabric bows, and twisted wire.

101

stand-up stars

stand-up stars patterns

What you need

Tracing paper
Pencil
½- to 1-inch-thick pine
Scissors
Band saw
Sandpaper
Tack cloth
Newspapers
Acrylic paints in desired colors
Paintbrush
Wood glue
Thick white crafts glue
Buttons
Fabric scraps
Wire and wire cutters
Round pencil, small dowel, or
  wooden skewer

What to do

1. Trace the desired star pattern, *opposite*, onto tracing paper. To trace the half-star pattern, first fold tracing paper in half. Align folds and trace star shape. Cut out shape and unfold tracing paper. Transfer the pattern to the wood.
2. Using a band saw, carefully cut on the pattern lines. Sand the edges until they are smooth. Wipe away dust from sanding using a tack cloth.
3. Cover your work area with newspapers. Using a desired color, paint one side and the edges of the star. Let the paint dry. Turn the star over and paint the other side. Let it dry. Apply second coats if needed. Let the paint dry.

4. Sand the edges of the star again to provide a weathered look. Remove any dust from sanding with a tack cloth.
5. If desired, layer a small star on top of a larger one, using the photograph on *pages 100–101* as a guide. Glue the stars together using wood glue. Let the glue dry.
6. For the button stars, use thick white crafts glue to affix a button to the center of the star. Let the glue dry. You can glue two or three buttons atop each other or glue several small buttons on the star if desired.
7. For the bow star, tear a narrow strip from fabric, approximately 1x12 inches. Place the fabric strip diagonally across the back of the star. Tie the fabric strip into a bow on the front side of the star. Glue the bow in place if desired. Trim the ends even.
8. For the wire-wrapped star, wrap a long length of wire around the center of the star as desired. Twist the wire ends together to secure. Trim the ends of the wire, leaving about 3 inches on each end. To make coiled ends, wrap the wire ends around a round pencil, small dowel, or wooden skewer. Remove the pencil or dowel. Shape the wires as desired.

Sources

- Purchase pine in crafts and home center stores and lumberyards.
- Vintage buttons are available at antiques stores and flea markets.

Woodworking tips

- To hang stars, add a screw eye in the top. Be sure to drill the hole first so the wood does not split.
- To give the stars a primitive look, sand the top surface as well as the edges.
- To mount the stars to the wall, attach sawtooth picture hangers to the back.
- When selecting pine for this project, choose pieces that are free of knots.

Cost to make project

50¢ to $2 per star, depending on the size

Suggested selling price

$2 to $8 per star, depending on the size and trims used

Time to make project

½ hour for a set of three

Timesaving tips

- Cut a pattern from cardboard so it can be traced around quickly.
- For a substitute for sandpaper, use an emery board or sanding block.
- To eliminate glue-drying time for the button embellished star, drill a hole in the center of the star and wire the button in place.
- Let kids sand the edges of the wooden stars.

TO SELL IT

- Sell the stars in sets of three.
- Attach a variety of trims: bows, twisted wire, buttons, jute, game pieces, beads, or other materials.

TO GIVE IT

- Place a set in a star-shaped box (or round if you can't find one to fit) and stamp the lid using a star stamp.
- Tie on a large jingle bell when giving these wood stars at Christmas.

just-for-dollies chairs

When dolls and teddy bears visit over tea,

these chairs will be perfect for the party.

Only 12½ inches high, these miniatures have

the same vintage look as any grown-up version.

What you need

Tracing paper and pencil
6x6-inch piece of ¾-inch
  pine wood for seat
Band saw; sandpaper
Drill with ¼ and ½-inch bits
Wood glue
Four ½-inch dowels, each
  5¼ inches long for legs
Two ¼-inch dowels, each
  4¼ inches long for leg braces
Two ¼-inch dowels, each
  3¾ inches long for leg braces
Two ¼-inch dowels, each
  6 inches long for back braces
Two ½-inch dowels, each
  7 inches long for back uprights
One ⅜-inch dowel, 5¼ inches
  long for back top rail
Acrylic paint in desired colors
Paintbrush

What to do

1. Enlarge and trace the seat pattern and drill marks, *right*, onto tracing paper. Transfer to 6x6-inch piece of wood. Carefully cut on line with a band saw. Sand edges until smooth.
2. Drill all holes ¼ inch into the seat. Drill holes in the bottom of the seat piece to insert the leg pieces, using a ½-inch bit. Drill these holes at slight angles toward the center of the seat. Drill holes on the top of the seat for the back brace and upright dowels using ¼- and ½-inch bits.
3. On all leg dowels, drill a ¼-inch hole 2⅝ inches from one end. Glue a 3¾-inch-long piece of ¼-inch dowel between two of the leg dowels. Repeat for the remaining pair of legs. These will form an "H" shape.
4. With the leg sections lying flat, drill ¼-inch holes 1½ inches from the bottom of each chair leg. Glue the legs into the holes in the seat. Glue 4¼-inch-long pieces of ¼-inch dowel to connect the leg sections. Let the glue dry.
5. Drill one ⅜-inch hole in each back upright, 1 inch from the end, halfway through for the back top rail. To connect the back top rail to the braces, drill two ¼-inch holes in the top rail, each 1⅝ inches from the end. Glue the brace pieces of dowel into the holes.
6. Glue the back uprights into the seat, adding the brace/rail piece. Adjust as needed and glue in place. Let the glue dry.
7. Paint the chair the desired color and let dry. Sand the edges for a vintage look.

Sources
- Look for wood dowels at home centers, crafts stores, hardware stores, and discount stores.
- Look for ¾-inch pine at home center stores.

Woodworking tips
- Wear safety glasses when using electric tools.
- To get a well-worn look, sand against the grain.

Cost to make project
Approximately $2

Suggested selling price
$15 for one chair

Time to make project
1 hour

Timesaving tips
- The chairs can be spray-painted with a matte paint, then sanded.
- Measure and cut several dowel pieces. Label the ends, if necessary.

TO SELL IT
- Use a variety of paint colors.
- Use purchased fabric coasters as cushions for those small chairs.

TO GIVE IT
- Place a doll or teddy bear on the chair when giving it to a child.
- Sign and date the bottom of the chair so its creator is known through generations.

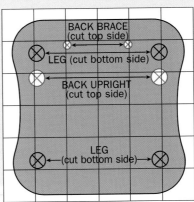

BACK BRACE
(cut top side)
LEG (cut bottom side)
BACK UPRIGHT
(cut top side)
LEG
(cut bottom side)

1 square = 1 inch

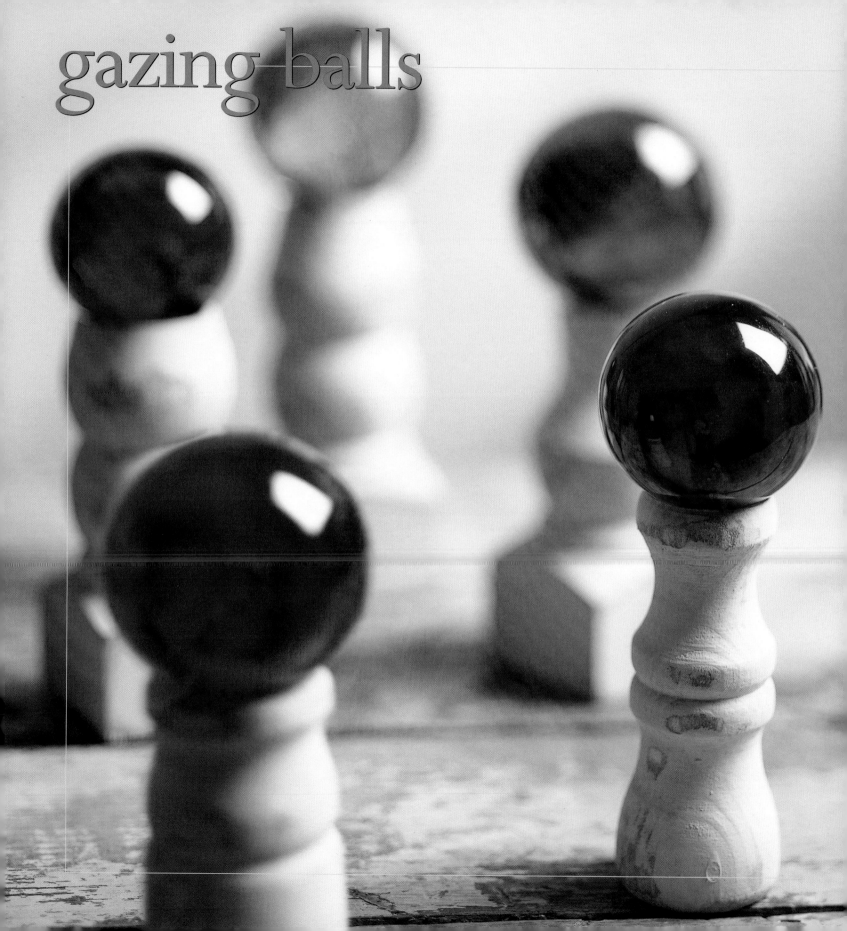

gazing balls

These miniature mirrors to the world add a glorious glimmer wherever they are displayed. The gazing balls are really holiday ornaments, and the stands are made from sections of wood staircase spindles. Small enough to hold in your hand, these tiny treasures are at home with a collection of potted plants, in a row on a windowsill, or grouped among candles for a centerpiece that is full of reflection.

What you need

Band saw
Staircase spindle
Sandpaper
Drill with 1-inch bit
Newspapers
Acrylic paints in desired colors
Paintbrush
Tack cloth
Glass Christmas ball
  ornament
Thick white crafts glue

What to do

1. Cut the desired length from the staircase spindle. Smooth any rough edges using sandpaper.
2. Decide which end of the spindle will be the top. Drill a 1-inch hole in the top to hold the ornament.
3. Cover your work surface with newspapers. Paint the spindle base the desired color using acrylic paint. You can paint the spindle a solid color, paint each section a different color, or paint tiny designs such as checks, stripes, dots, flowers, or hearts. Let the paint dry thoroughly.
4. Sand the edges of the spindle to achieve a worn effect. Remove any dust from sanding by wiping with a tack cloth.
5. Carefully remove the hanger topper from the ball ornament. Glue the top of the ornament into the hole in the spindle. Let the glue dry.

Sources
- Purchase spindles in home centers.
- Look for Christmas balls in department, gift, and crafts stores.

Woodworking tips
- If you don't have sandpaper on hand, you can use an emery board for small sanding jobs.
- Another way to make a base for these miniature gazing balls is by gluing together wood parts such as round and square beads, candle cups, and thread spools. Using this method, you may not have to drill a hole in the top to place the ornament.

Cost to make project
$2

Suggested selling price
$6 to $10, depending on size and intricacy of painting

Time to make project
15 to 30 minutes

Timesaving tips
- Spray-paint the spindle bases instead of using a paintbrush.
- Make several gazing balls in stages.
- If you can find vintage painted spindles, you can simply cut them into the size you want, and this will eliminate the painting step altogether.

TO SELL IT
- Display the gazing balls among silk flowers and miniature fences.
- Make coordinating gazing balls at different heights to encourage customers to make multiple purchases.

TO GIVE IT
- Personalize the gazing balls by writing a message, date, or friend's name on the spindle base.
- To give a miniature gazing ball, place it in a planter and fill with packages of flower or herb seeds.

cutout coasters

Familiar shapes pair with practicality in the making of these clever wooden coasters. Perfect for a game-playing gathering or afternoon tea, these useful pieces sell well in sets.

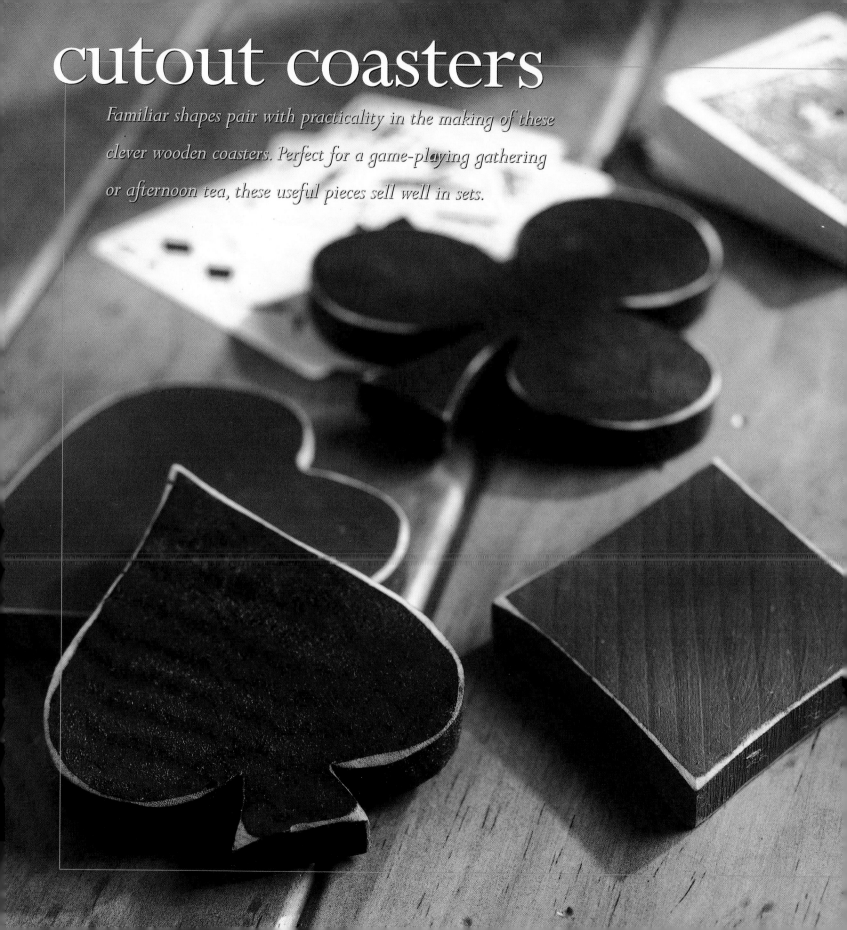

cutout coasters

teapot coaster and trivet patterns

dice coasters

(As shown on page 109)

What you need

½-inch pine; table saw
Medium sandpaper
Pencil; ruler
Drill press and 60-degree
  router bit or 1-inch drill bit
Acrylic paints in cream
  and black; paintbrush
Acrylic crafts spray

What to do

1. For one set, cut six
3½x3½-inch squares from
½-inch pine. Sand the edges.
2. Paint the squares with
cream paint. Let the paint
dry thoroughly.
3. Using the placement
diagrams on *page 113* as a
guide, measure and mark
where dots will appear on each
coaster. Mark dots one through
six as on dice. The center
holes on one, three, and five
are in the center of each
square. The remainder of the
dots are ¾ inch from the edges.
4. Use a router bit or drill
bit to make indentations
where dots are marked.
Paint the indentations black.
If you wish to eliminate
using a drill, the dots can
simply be painted, using a
dowel end dipped in paint.
5. Sand the edges of the
coasters if desired. Spray
the tops and sides using
acrylic crafts spray.

What you need

Pencil and tracing paper
½-inch pine
Scroll saw or bandsaw
Medium sandpaper

Acrylic paints in black and red
Paintbrush
Acrylic crafts spray

card set coasters

(As shown on page 108)

What to do

1. Trace patterns, *pages
112–113*, onto tracing paper.
Transfer patterns to pine. Cut
out shapes and sand the edges.
2. Paint the club and spade
shapes black. Paint the
diamond and heart shapes
red. Let the paint dry.
3. Sand the edges of the
coasters if desired. Spray
the tops and sides using
acrylic crafts spray.

teapot coasters and trivet

(As shown on page 109)

What you need

Pencil and tracing paper
½-inch pine
Scroll saw or bandsaw
Medium sandpaper
Acrylic paints in red, blue, and
  yellow or other desired colors
Acrylic crafts spray

What to do

1. Trace the patterns,
opposite, onto tracing paper.
Transfer patterns to pine.
Cut out as many shapes as
desired and sand the edges.
2. Paint the teapot shapes as
desired. Let the paint dry.
3. Sand the edges if desired.
Spray the tops and sides
using acrylic crafts spray.

Sources

- Purchase lengths of
  ½-inch pine in home center
  stores, crafts stores, and
  discount stores.
- Purchase a bandsaw or
  scroll saw in home center
  stores, hardware stores, or
  discount stores.

Woodworking tips

- Be sure to wear protective
  eyewear when using electric
  tools such as a scroll saw,
  bandsaw, or table saw.
- To get vivid colors when
  painting on wood, you may
  want to base-coat the wood
  with a primer before
  applying the color. You can
  also paint more than one
  coat of color.

Cost to make project

$1 a set

Suggested selling price

$10 to 15 per set of four,
$8 for a single teapot trivet

Time to make project

45 minutes to 1 hour per
set of 4

Timesaving tips

- Instead of drilling the dots
  on the dice, paint them
  using a dowel end dipped
  in paint.
- For the teapot coasters
  and trivet, eliminate a
  time-consuming cut in the
  wood by painting the area
  between the handle and the
  pot instead.

TO SELL IT

- Bundle sets together and
  tie with coordinating ribbons.

- Display a list of possible
  gift recipients, such as
  members of a card club,
  teachers, or neighbors.

TO GIVE IT

- Wrap the card set
  coasters with a box
  of playing cards.
- Paint a polka-dot set

of clear coffee mugs
to tuck into a gift basket
with the teapot coasters
and trivet.

cutout coasters

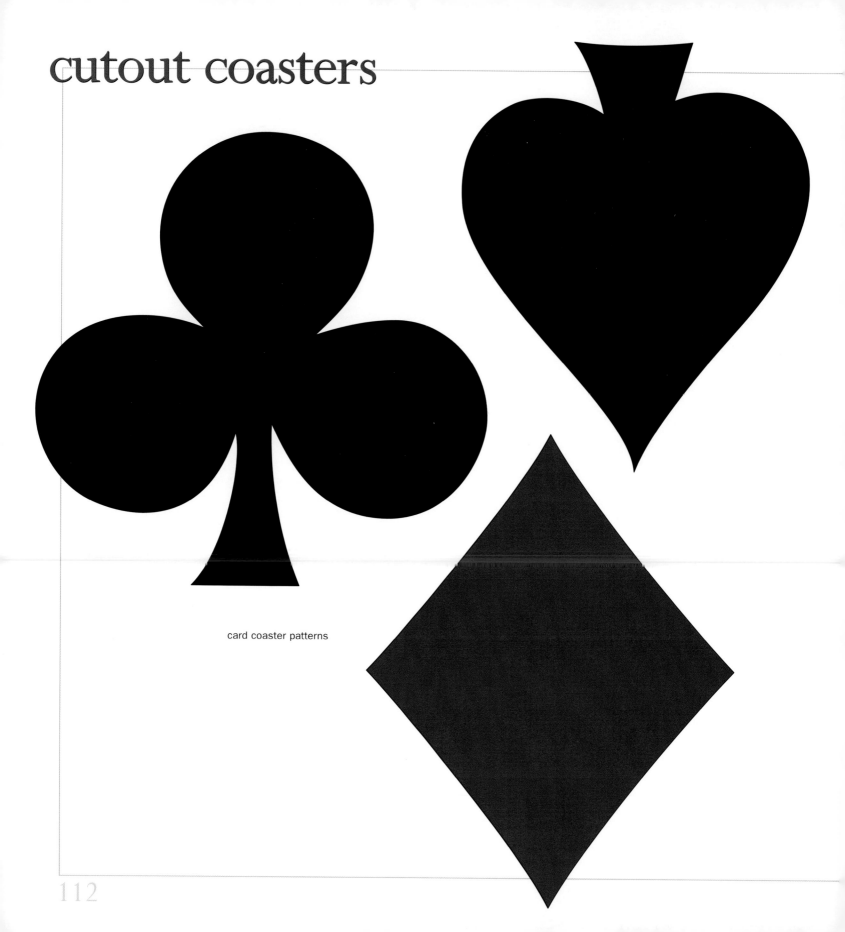

card coaster patterns

dice coaster
indentation diagram

rolling pin birdhouses

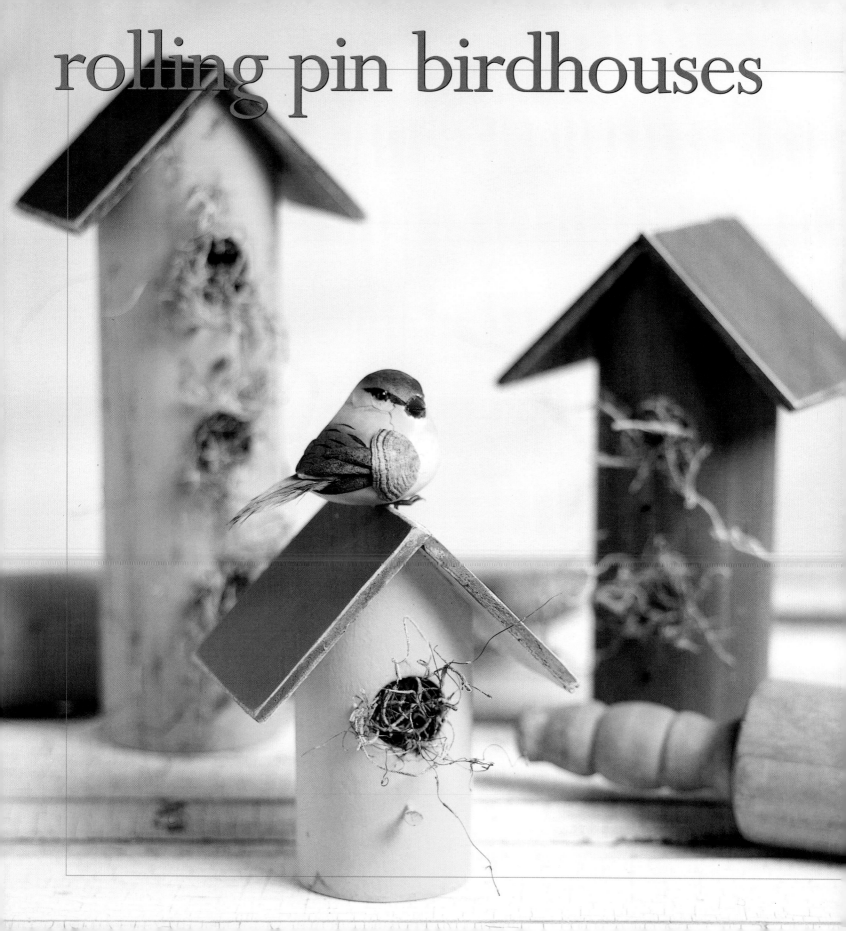

Who would have guessed these decorative birdhouses once resided in the kitchen drawer? Made from well-used rolling pins, the birdhouses are painted in country colors and have plywood roofs. Try these same techniques on stairway spindles, or even chair and table legs.

What you need

Rolling pin
Table saw
Tape measure
Pencil
Drill and 1-inch bit
Hammer
Small flathead nails
Plywood
Wood glue
Acrylic paints in desired colors
Paintbrush
Medium sandpaper
Moss
Thick white crafts glue
Artificial bird

What to do

1. Saw off one end of the rolling pin. This will be the bottom of the birdhouse. Decide how tall you want the birdhouse. Mark the desired height on the rolling pin. Cut the marked end at a 45-degree angle. This will be the roof end.
2. For the entrances, drill the desired number of 1-inch holes along one side of the rolling pin. For perches, hammer in nails just below drilled holes.
3. For the roof, cut a 3-inch-wide strip of ¼-inch plywood into two pieces, 3x3½ and 3x3¼ inches. Use wood glue to adhere these pieces to the angled roof cuts on the rolling pin with the shorter piece butting against the longer one as shown in the photo, *opposite.* Let the glue dry.
4. Using the photograph *opposite,* as a guide, paint the birdhouse, using the desired colors of acrylic paint. Let the paint dry. To create a weathered look on the birdhouse, sand the edges of the roof and entrance holes as well as any other desired surfaces.
5. Add small bunches of moss in entrance holes. Using crafts glue, attach a bird to the roof peak or one of the nail perches, if desired.

Sources
- Look for rolling pins in discount stores, flea markets, or in garage sales.
- Purchase plywood in crafts stores and home center stores.

Woodworking tips
- When using electric tools, such as a saw or drill, wear protective eyewear.
- To drill holes that are perfectly aligned, measure and mark carefully using a ruler.

Cost to make project
$3 to $5 per birdhouse

Suggested selling price
$6 to $18 per birdhouse

Time to make project
½ to 1 hour

Timesaving tips
- Instead of making the roof cuts at 45-degree angles, make one angled cut. This saves on cuts, and the roof piece can be one piece of plywood instead of two.
- Use spray paint instead of acrylic paint. If a contrasting roof color is desired, paint it using a brush.

TO SELL IT
- Make coordinating birdhouses in different heights to encourage multiple sales.
- Advertise that houses can be used as decoration only, indoors or out. You may want to spray with acrylic sealer if they are to be put outside.

TO GIVE IT
- Give a set of three coordinating birdhouses as a housewarming or birthday gift.
- For a more contemporary look, don't sand the edges after painting. Add painted patterns, such as spirals, checks, and stripes.

playful plant pokes

Trimmed with colorful wires and stickers that look like old-fashioned seed packets, these fun plant pokes brighten any windowsill. Because they take minutes to make, you can whip up an entire collection in an evening.

playful plant pokes

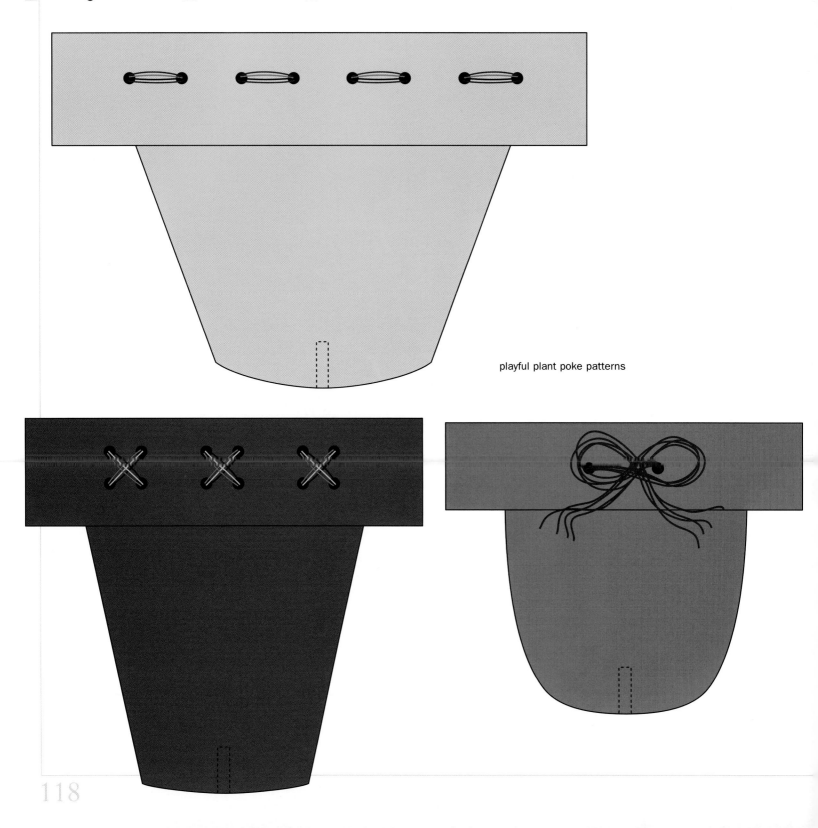

playful plant poke patterns

What you need

Tracing paper and pencil
½- and ⅛-inch pine
Ruler
Band saw
Medium sandpaper
Wood glue
Drill and ⅛-inch drill bit
Acrylic paints in desired colors
Paintbrush
18-gauge wire
Seed packet or other stickers
Varnish, if desired

What to do

1. Trace the desired pattern from *pages 118, 120,* and *121.* Transfer the large flowerpot pattern (with rim) to the ½-inch pine and the rim only to the ⅛-inch pine. Cut out the shapes and sand the edges.

2. Glue the ⅛-inch rim piece on top of the ½-inch flowerpot shape. Let the glue dry.

3. Drill a hole in the center of the plant poke bottom. If you wish to add wire to the rim area, drill holes through the rim using the patterns as guides.

4. Paint the wood shapes with the desired color of paint. Let the paint dry. Apply a second coat if needed. Let it dry. Sand the edges of the painted wood for a worn appearance.

5. Using the photograph on *pages 116–117* for inspiration, lace wire through the drilled holes in the rim.

6. Apply a sticker to the plant poke front. Apply a coat of varnish, if desired. Let the varnish dry.

7. Firmly push the armature wire into the bottom hole. Bend the wire into a spiral, zigzag, or other desired shape.

Sources

- Purchase pine for crafting in home center, crafts, and discount stores.
- Purchase a band saw or scroll saw in home center, hardware, or discount stores. Be sure to read the safety instructions before using, and wear protective eyewear.

Woodworking tip

- When gluing pieces of wood together, use a clamp or heavy rubber bands to hold them in place until the glue is dry.

Cost to make project

75¢ per plant poke

Suggested selling price

$4 for one, $10 for three

Time to make project

20 minutes

Timesaving tips

- Make several of the same-shape plant pokes at once, using the same wiring design, paint color, and sticker shape.
- Eliminate the ⅛-inch piece of pine added to the rim.
- Use a straight piece of wire or dowel in place of the shaped support wire.

TO SELL IT

- Display your works of art poked into the dirt in potted plants.
- Display a list of possible gift recipients, such as members of a gardening club, teachers, neighbors, or coworkers.

TO GIVE IT

- Place a plant poke or two in a flowering plant to brighten someone's day.
- Place a set of plant pokes in a watering can and

instead of stickers, leave a place to write in names of flowers or veggies to be used as garden markers.

playful plant pokes

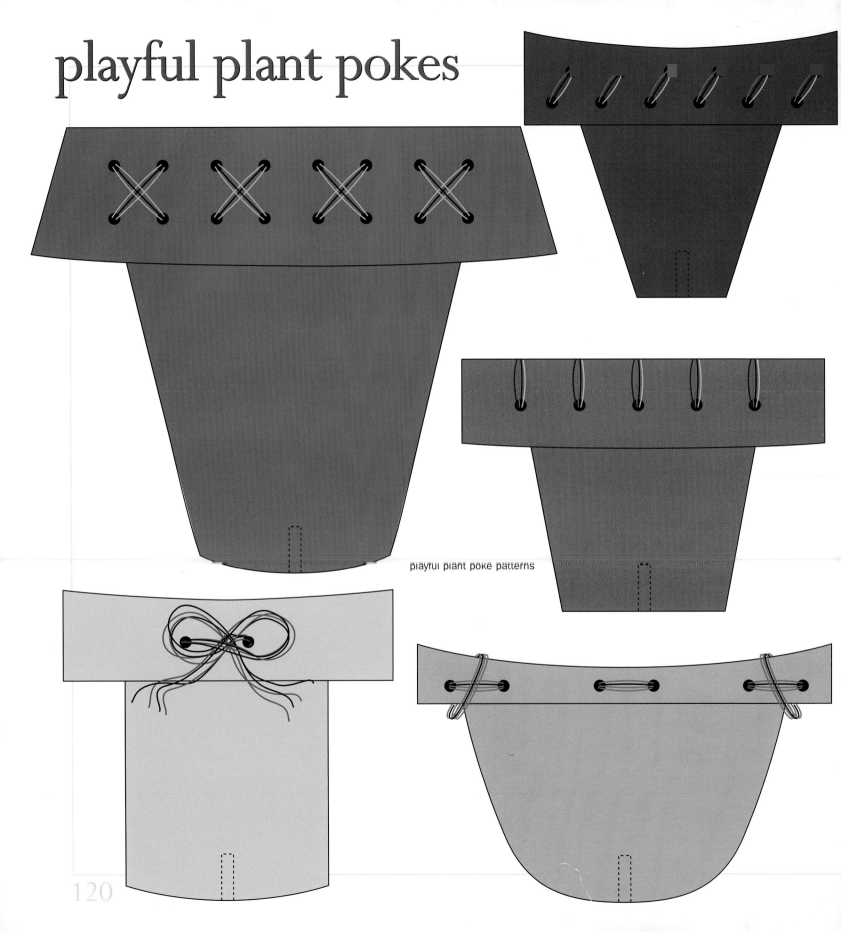

playful plant poke patterns

playful plant poke patterns

kids' play flowers

These perky flowers are sure to bring out the kid in everyone! Made from painted wood toy pieces, this variety doesn't need watering and is in bloom year-round. Use the playful flowers as plant pokes or group them together in a pot for a fun artificial arrangement. Displayed in a kid's room, or any spot where a childlike touch is enjoyed, these quick-to-make posies are guaranteed to bring smiles.

What you need
Wood toy pieces
½-inch dowels
Saw
Newspapers
Acrylic paints in desired colors
Paintbrush
Wood glue
Flowerpot and rocks, if desired

What to do
1. Select the toy pieces to shape a flower with seven petals, one stem, and one round center piece. To make the small center piece, cut a ⅛-inch piece from the wooden dowel.

2. Cover your work area with newspapers. Using the photograph, *opposite*, for inspiration, paint all of the pieces in the desired colors. Let the paint dry.
3. Assemble the flower by firmly pushing the toy pieces together. Glue the pieces in place if desired. Glue the short dowel piece in the center of the flower. Let the glue dry.
4. If selling the flowers as an arrangement, place five or more stems into a rock-filled flowerpot. Separate the flowers and adjust them to be displayed at different heights.

Sources
- Look for wood toy pieces like these in game and toy stores.
- Purchase dowels in discount, home center, and crafts stores.

Woodworking tips
- If you can't find wood toy pieces like these, check the precut wood pieces in a crafts store. You may have to drill holes, but the outcome will look similar.
- If any wood glue oozes from the joints when assembling the flowers, wipe it away with a damp paper towel before it dries.

Cost to make project
10¢ per flower

Suggested selling price
$1 per flower

Time to make project
10 minutes per flower

Timesaving tips
- To make painting quick, make several flowers of the same color at the same time.
- Stick the ends of the straight pieces into a block of plastic foam when painting. If using dowels for the stems and petals, paint them before cutting into the desired lengths.
- Cut a dowel into several short pieces to make the centers of the flowers.

TO SELL IT
- Sell one at a time or by the dozen, just like the fresh-cut variety.
- Advertise the different ways to use these flowers.

List plant pokes, decorations, package trims, garden markers, bookmarks—even rulers when you add measurement marks to the stem.

TO GIVE IT
- Place several flowers in a pot and secure with sand, marbles, or rocks.
- Tie a flower to a bow on a package to give as a plant poke.

IT'S
ALWAYS
CHRISTMAS

During the blessed Christmas season, handcrafted gifts

provide heartfelt joy to the crafter as well as the recipient.

This chapter of festive projects will convey the loving

spirit of the holidays. From tiny tree trims and jolly cookie

jars to tassels made with traditional holiday hues, you'll be

inspired to craft for Christmas any time of the year.

MERRY IN THE MAKING

Making Projects for Christmas

The magic of the holidays always seems to bring crafts lovers out in droves. Whether they are searching for something special for their own holiday home or looking for handcrafted gifts to give with heartfelt sentiments, this eager crowd will be on the lookout for new creative pieces to celebrate the wonderful Christmas season.

People often purchase multiples to give to card club members, teachers, coworkers, etc. So if you're selling gift items, it's a good idea to have several duplicate projects available. And if there's enough time before Christmas, and you are able, be sure to indicate on a sign that you will take special orders for certain items.

Selling Christmas Items

Pricing is very important during the holiday season. First, crafters have much competition—from the flood of other bazaars to the many stores that beckon holiday shoppers. People also have many gifts to buy, so they scrutinize and compare prices. It may take a few years to see what works best for you—a handful of one-of-a-kind pieces with intricate work that carry a high price tag or dozens of quick-to-make projects that sell for under $10. Anticipate your audience and keep an eye on what sells at each show. Shoppers in different areas of the country have different tastes, budgets, and purchasing habits.

While traditional red and green are always popular, some people prefer burgundy and emerald green. This slight color variation may help you get a sale you might otherwise have missed.

To make ordinary price tags more festive, simply stamp one side of the tag using a holiday-themed rubber stamp and red or green ink. Little touches like this will help create a fun atmosphere at your booth or table.

To draw customers to your creations, make your display stand out among the others. Depending on the location and restrictions of the show, you may be able to add a warm glow to your table or booth by using holiday lights and fabrics, or by playing joyous music. Would a bowl of tiny candy canes draw customers? Do you need a tree on which to hang ornaments or other small items? Is your name (or that of your company) front and center so repeat customers can find you? Make it easy for shoppers to locate you and select items they wish to purchase.

Since many Christmas shoppers will be buying gift items, have boxes and packing materials on hand so you can wrap the purchases easily. If you have enough help and space, this may be a service you could offer at the show for an additional fee.

old-fashioned trims

Pieced felt joined by delicate stitches lends a country feel to these tiny treasures. Hang these holiday creations alone as ornaments or string them together for a charming garland on the mantel or banister.

What you need

Tracing or typing paper
Pencil
Scissors
Pins
Felt in desired colors
Fabric glue
Embroidery floss in a color to contrast felt colors
Needle
Assorted holiday buttons and charms, including two star buttons
Three 8-inch-long pieces of ¼-inch ribbon
Fiberfill

What to do

1. Trace the patterns on *pages 130–131* onto tracing or typing paper. Cut out the pattern pieces. Pin the patterns to the desired colors of felt. Cut out the crazy quilt felt shapes. Cut two of the background.
2. Arrange the crazy pieces on top of one background piece with no space between pieces. Glue the crazy pieces in place.
3. Using three plies of embroidery floss, stitch over the seams using a herringbone stitch as shown on *page 131*. Stitch around the edges with a running stitch. Use a floss color that contrasts with the felt color.
4. Sew on all buttons (except the star buttons) and charms (see the photographs, *opposite and right,* for placement ideas).
5. Pin the crazy quilt unit on top of the remaining background piece. Fold each ribbon piece in half. Put the ends between the two background pieces. Center the ribbon for the tree and heart and put in the right corner for the stocking.
6. Stitch the edges of the ivory pieces together using blanket stitches, stopping 2 inches from the beginning stitch. Stuff the ornaments with fiberfill, then continue with the blanket stich.
7. Sew the star buttons to the top of the tree and the top right corner of the stocking as shown in the photograph.

Sources
- Purchase felt, charms, and buttons in crafts, fabric, and discount stores.

Crafting tips
- To make embroidery stitches lie flat, separate all plies of embroidery floss, then recombine the three plies needed.
- When sewing decorative stitches with embroidery floss, use a sharp needle with a large eye.
- To use the stockings as small gift "wraps" instead of ornaments, leave the top edge open to insert a tiny package, gift certificate, or money.
- Use paint or marker to make faux stitches.

Cost to make project
$2 per ornament

Suggested selling price
$8 for one, a pair for $15

Time to make project
1 hour

Timesaving tips
- To make stitching easier, keep the glue away from the seams where the decorative stitching will appear.
- Cut several 3-ply lengths of embroidery floss to have ready for stitching.

TO SELL IT
- Sell in sets of three at a discounted price.
- Make some of the stockings into gift holders as described above in Crafting tips.

TO GIVE IT
- Enlarge the stocking pattern and adjust the finishing to make a stocking large enough for St. Nick to fill.
- Select meaningful charms to sew on the trims, such as an apple for a teacher or ballet slippers for a dancer.

old-fashioned trims

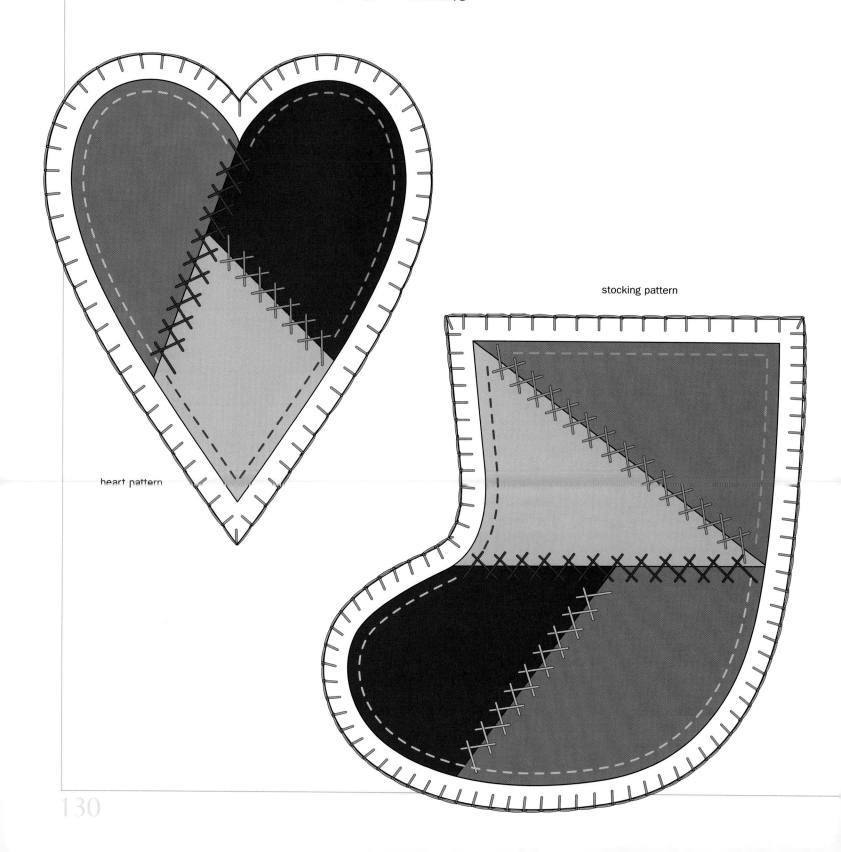

heart pattern

stocking pattern

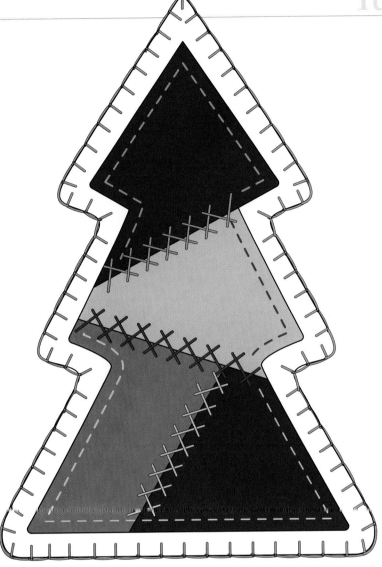

tree pattern

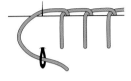

blanket stitch

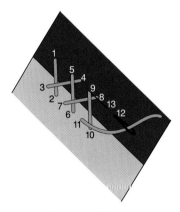

herringbone stitch

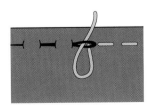

running stitch

holiday treat jars

merry christmas
cookies jar

These bright jars are perfect for the season's sweet surprises. Adaptable to any jar shape, mix and match these designs as you like.

candy cane stripe
treat jar

gingerbread man
cookie jar

trimmed tree
candy jar

holiday treat jars

gingerbread man cookie jar

(As shown on page 133)

What you need

Glass jar with lid
Newspapers
Tracing or typing paper
Pencil
Scissors
Tape
Disposable foam plate
*Acrylic glass paints in
    green, white, red, brown,
    and black*
Paintbrush

What to do

1. Before beginning to paint, wash the glassware and let it dry. Be careful not to touch the areas that will be painted.
2. Cover your work surface with newspapers. Trace the pattern, *right,* onto tracing or typing paper. (If necessary, reduce or enlarge the pattern on a copy machine to fit your jar.) Trim any extra paper away from the design. Tape the pattern to the inside of the candy jar.
3. On a foam plate, mix a small amount of green paint with white paint to make light mint green. Paint the background shape, going around the shape for the gingerbread man. While the paint is wet, add a few swirls of white paint. Paint the lid with the light mint

green paint. Highlight with white. Let the paint dry.
4. Paint the gingerbread man brown. Let the paint dry. Paint in the details of the gingerbread man, the background, and the lid. To mix pink tones, stir a dab of red paint into white without mixing completely. To make dots, dip the handle end of a paintbrush into the desired color of paint and dot on the surface. Let the paint dry.

candy cane stripe treat jar

(As shown on page 133)

What you need

Round glass jar with lid
Newspapers
Disposable foam plate
*Acrylic glass paints in red,
    white, and green*
*¼- and 1-inch-wide flat
    paintbrushes*
Pencil with round-tip eraser
Toothpick

What to do

1. Before beginning to paint, wash the glassware and let it dry. Be careful not to touch the areas that will be painted.

gingerbread man cookie jar pattern

2. Cover your work surface with newspapers. Place some white paint on a foam plate. Using the ¼-inch brush, paint a ring around the top of the jar and on the edge of the lid knob. Using the 1-inch-wide brush, paint slanted stripes around the jar, leaving about 2 inches between stripes. Let dry.
3. Paint 1-inch red stripes between the white stripes. Use the ¼-inch brush to paint vertical stripes over the white-painted rings at top and on knob. Let the paint dry.
4. To add green dots to the jar and lid, dip the eraser end of a pencil into paint and dot on the surface.

Let the paint dry. To add tiny white and red dots in the center of the larger green dots, use a toothpick dipped in paint.
5. Paint the knob top red. Let the paint dry. To add white dots on the top of the knob, dip the handle end of a paintbrush into paint and dot on the knob. Let the paint dry.

trimmed tree candy jar
(As shown on page 133)

What you need
Glass jar with lid
Newspapers
Disposable foam plate
Acrylic glass paints in green, white, purple, dark green, metallic gold, red, and yellow
Paintbrushes
Toothpick
Old toothbrush

What to do
1. Before beginning to paint, wash the glassware and let it dry. Be careful not to touch the areas that will be painted.
2. Cover your work surface with newspapers. On the plate, mix a small amount of green with white. Start to paint the snow at the bottom of the jar. Using the same colors, paint a large tree on each side of the jar. Mix a small amount of purple with white and continue painting the top of the snow. Let the paint dry.
3. Using dark green, paint small trees around the jar between the large trees. Add stars to the top of each large tree using metallic gold. Paint various size stars on the lid. Let the paint dry.

4. To add trims to the large trees, dip the handle end of a paintbrush into the desired colors of paint and dot on trees. For garlands, use a toothpick and gold paint. Make several dots in a row. Let the paint dry.
5. Dip the bristles of an old toothbrush into white paint. Run your finger along the bristles to splatter specks of paint over the jar to resemble snow. Let the paint dry.

merry christmas cookies jar
(As shown on page 132)

What you need
Glass jar with lid
Newspapers
Tracing or typing paper
Scissors
Pencil with round-tip eraser
Tape
Etching cream
Rubber gloves
Small round, fine-tipped, and ½-inch flat paintbrushes
Disposable foam plate
Acrylic glass paints in red, white, green, teal, purple, and silver
Red metallic cord
3 medium jingle bells

continued on page 136

Sources
- Look for glass jars at flea markets, garage sales, discount stores, and home accessory stores.
- Purchase glass paints and etching cream at crafts and art stores.

Crafting tips
- The glass paint you choose may require baking to become permanent. Be sure to read the paint label.
- Be very careful when using etching cream. Read all of the directions on the label and be sure to keep away from children.
- Use the motifs on the glassware as inspiration for gift tags

Cost to make project
Approximately $1 to $8 per jar

Suggested selling price
$6 to $20, depending on size of jar and the intricacy of the painted design

Time to make project
45 minutes to 1 hour

Timesaving tips
- Use the dishwasher to wash the jars before beginning to paint.
- Make photocopies of your drawn patterns so you can work on many jars at the same time without having to trace the pattern several times.
- Paint several similarly shaped jars at the same time using the same design.

TO SELL IT
- Provide a card with each jar that states the paint is permanent but hand washing is recommended.
- Wrap the lids and bottoms separately in bubble wrap before bagging. (Do not wrap in newspaper as the print may rub off.)

TO GIVE IT
- Tie a fresh sprig of holly or evergreen around the lid.
- Fill the jar with fresh-baked cookies or holiday candies.

135

holiday treat jars

What to do for the merry christmas jar

1. Before beginning to paint, wash the jar and let it dry. Be careful not to touch the areas to be painted.

◀ **2.** Cover your work surface with newspapers. Trace the pattern, *page 137*, onto tracing or typing paper. Trim any extra paper away from the design. (If necessary, reduce or enlarge the pattern on a copy machine to fit your jar.) Tape the pattern to the inside of the candy jar.

▼ **3.** Using etching cream, paint the words on the outside of the jar as shown by the pattern. Be very careful, as the glass will etch wherever the cream is applied. Read the directions on the etching cream label to know how long to let the cream stay on the glass.

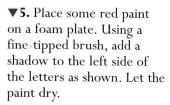

▲ **4.** Put on the rubber gloves. When the time is up for the etching cream, rinse off the cream under the faucet. Dry the jar.

▼ **5.** Place some red paint on a foam plate. Using a fine-tipped brush, add a shadow to the left side of the letters as shown. Let the paint dry.

▲ **6.** Add white highlights to the top of each letter. Let the paint dry.

▶ **7.** Place green, teal, and white paints on a disposable plate. Drag the flat brush through each color and begin to add sprigs of greenery around the lettering and the jar lid. Start from the center of the sprig and brush outward. Continue making these strokes until you have the length of sprig desired. Let the paint dry.

8. Add red berries by dipping the eraser end of a pencil into red paint and dotting it on the surface. To add garlands, use this same method using desired colors of paint mixed with white. Let the paint dry.

9. String three jingle bells onto the cord. Tie around the lid knob.

merry christmas cookies

merry christmas cookies jar pattern

137

festive tassels

Whether hung from a doorknob, tree branch, or a drawer pull, these elegant tassels add a touch of holiday flair. The cording-covered toppers are really wood shapes underneath, making a sturdy form to wrap in the colors of the season.

What to do for all tassels

1. Start wrapping at the top of the tassel and wrap down, with the wraps tight against each other. Spread adhesive with a crafts stick over 1 inch at the top of the wood area to be wrapped. Work in 1-inch segments of gluing and wrapping.

2. If there is a hole at the top of the wood piece you are using, fold a 4½-inch hanger loop at one end of the cord. Stick the ends of the loop in the hole and bring out the end with the remainder of the cord. Glue to the inside of the hole and use the remaining cord to wrap.

3. You will have to hide the end of a cord under a wrap when there is no hole at the top of the wood piece or when you are changing colors of cord. Untwist ⅓ inch of cord and spread flat. Glue the end in the area below the top wrap, then wrap on top of the end. If you are making a hanger, leave a 4-inch loop prior to starting the wrap.

4. Continue wrapping and gluing until you get to the bottom of the rim.

red and green tassel

What you need

4½-inch wood curtain rod finial
Permanent fabric adhesive
Scissors
3 yards red twisted cord
1½ yards green rattail cord
16-inch piece of 5-inch-long green bullion fringe
Ten ⅜-inch red buttons

continued on page 140

Sources
- Look for wooden pieces for toppers in the wood section of crafts and discount stores.
- Find fringe, braid, and cording in fabric and discount stores.

Crafting tip
- Craft glues that are thick work well for this project because they do not drip and they grip the cord and fringe immediately so the materials do not slide.

Cost to make project
$2 to $5 per tassel

Suggested selling price
$7 to $14, depending on size of tassel and materials used

Time to make project
½ hour

Timesaving tip
- Cut materials for several tassels to be made at the same time.

TO SELL IT
- Display a list of places these tassels can be used, such as doors and drawers.
- Make tassels in other seasonal colors so customers can change their trims throughout the year.

TO GIVE IT
- Tie a tassel to the top of a package as a bow.
- Gently wrap the tassel in tissue to keep the fringes in place.

festive tassels

▲ **3.** Then continue wrapping with red cord.
▶ **4.** Wrap and glue two layers of 5-inch green bullion fringe around the bottom edge of the finial.

What to do for the red and green tassel
▲ **1.** Make a 4-inch loop at the top of the finial and wrap and glue red cord to the bottom of the neck area of the finial.
▶ **2.** Wrap and glue green rattail cording around the widest part of the finial.

▲ **5.** Glue the red buttons around the top of the bullion fringe, spacing the buttons ⅓ inch apart.

gold and red tassel

What you need

Standard size wooden candle cup
4 yards metallic gold cord
12-inch piece of 4-inch-long red fringe
Permanent fabric adhesive
Beading needle
Green quilting thread
28 green silver-lined rochailles beads
14 gold silver-lined rochailles beads
Seven ¼-inch-wide green glass beads
Glass seed beads in emerald green
Scissors

What to do

1. Make a 4-inch loop at the top of the candle cup and wrap and glue metallic gold cord around the cup. Glue end of wrap inside the candle cup.
2. Roll red fringe and glue fringe together along top edge as you roll. Glue the top edge of the fringe to the inside of the candle cup.

3. Using beading needle and green thread, make seven strings of beaded fringe around the base of the candle cup, spacing beaded strings ⅓ inch apart. To make the fringe, secure end of thread in the red fringe. Come out at the base of the candle cup and string two green rochailles beads, one gold rochailles bead, two green rochailles beads, one gold rochailles bead, one 1¼-inch-wide green bead and one green seed bead. Bring the needle back through the ¼-inch-wide green bead and the remaining beads, skipping the seed bead. Put needle back through red fringe to secure thread and come put ⅓ inch away to begin a new string of beads. Continue around base of candle cup. Secure the end of the thread inside the red fringe.

green and gold bullion tassel

What you need

2½-inch wood bean pot
Permanent fabric adhesive
4½ yards green rattail cord
12-inch piece of 5-inch-long green bullion fringe
6-inch piece of metallic gold 2½-inch bullion fringe
8 inches of ⅝-inch-wide red flat braid
Scissors

What to do

1. Turn the bean pot so that the open area is at the bottom. Make a 4-inch loop using green rattail cord and glue to the top of the bean pot and wrap and glue the green rattail cord around the bean pot. Glue end of cord inside open edge of bean pot.
2. Roll the 5-inch piece of green bullion fringe and glue along top edge as you wrap. Check as you wrap for the fit of the roll inside the bean pot, stopping before it gets very snug. Wrap and glue one layer of metallic gold bullion on top of the green bullion fringe. Glue top edge of fringe roll inside the bead pot.
3. Glue the flat red braid along the bottom edge of the wrapped bean pot.

ready for santa set

Kids will love setting out cookies and milk for St. Nick on this matching snack set. The fun part is shopping for mix-and-match glassware to etch with Santa's initial.

What you need
Clear glass plate
Clear glass tumbler or mug
Tracing or typing paper
Pencil
Contact paper
Cardboard
Crafts knife
Etching cream
Small round paintbrush
Rubber gloves

What to do
1. Before beginning, wash the glassware and let it dry.
2. Trace the S patterns, *right* and *below*. Transfer each pattern to the paper side of a small piece of Contact paper approximately 1 inch larger than the pattern. Without removing the backing, place the pieces of Contact paper on cardboard. Use a crafts knife to carefully remove each S. Discard the S shapes.
3. Stick the Contact paper square with the small S onto the tumbler. Stick the large S on the back of the plate. Press all edges firmly to the glass.
4. Use a paintbrush to paint etching cream over the S shapes. Apply etching cream to plate rim and tumbler foot, if desired. Follow the instructions on the etching cream label to determine how long to leave on the cream.
5. When the time is up, put on rubber gloves. Carefully rinse off the cream under the faucet. Let the pieces dry.

S

plate pattern

Sources
■ Purchase mix-and-match glassware at flea markets, garage sales, discount stores, and home accessory stores.
■ Purchase etching cream at crafts and art stores.

Crafting tips
■ To ensure the S shapes are crisp, press the Contact paper onto the glassware using a crafts stick.
■ Be very careful when using etching cream. Read all of the directions on the label and be sure to keep away from children.

Cost to make project
$1 to $4 per set

Suggested selling price
$10 to $18, depending on glassware used

Time to make project
15 minutes to ½ hour

Timesaving tip
■ Use glass paint to freehand the S.

S

tumbler pattern

TO SELL IT
■ Place a Christmas cookie on the display plate with a note to Santa.
■ When sold, wrap each piece of glassware separately in bubble wrap before placing in a bag.

TO GIVE IT
■ Place cookies on the plate and hot chocolate mix in the cup for gift giving.
■ To give to a child, add a pen and holiday paper so a note can be left for Santa.

143

joyful ornaments

Simplicity says it all with these flower-topped ornaments. Using quick-to-do techniques, you can make the whole collection the night before Christmas.

beribboned ornaments

metallic stars

beaded coil trim

joy to the world
ornament

joyful ornaments

snowflakes-
all-around
ornaments

joy-to-the-world ornament
(As shown on page 145)

What you need

White ball ornament
Pencil
Newspapers
Glass paints in red and white
Paintbrushes
14-inch piece of $^7/_8$-inch-wide
   red velvet ribbon
28-inch piece of $1^1/_4$-inch-wide
   white sheer ribbon
Hot-glue gun and hot glue

What to do

1. Using the pattern as a guide, lightly write the word "joy" in script across the front of the ornament using pencil.
2. Cover the work surface with newspapers. Carefully paint over the lettering using red paint. Let it dry thoroughly. Highlight the

joy-to-the-world ornament pattern

tops of the letters with tiny strokes of white paint. Let the paint dry.
3. Tie a bow with the red ribbon. Cut an 18-inch piece from white ribbon. Begin to tie a bow with the white ribbon, placing the red bow in the center before wrapping the center of the white bow. Tie the bow tightly.
4. Knot the ends of the remaining piece of white ribbon. From the front of the ornament, pull the loop of the ribbon through to the knot. Glue the bow on top of the knot. Fold the ends of the ribbon and cut at a slant to make finished ends.

beaded coil trim
(As shown on page 145)

What you need

Armature wire or lead-free
   solder
Wire cutter
Needlenose pliers
Silver beading wire
Four large beads in
   desired colors
Five 18mm silver beads
$^1/_2$-inch-wide silver ribbon

What to do

1. Cut a 36-inch piece of armature wire or solder

using a wire cutter. Beginning at one end, use a needlenose pliers to make a tiny circle. Continue wrapping the wire until the coil is about the size of a dime. This will be the ornament top.
2. Bring the wire down to form an oval that is about 3 inches high. Continue forming the wire into smaller ovals; keep the wires close at the top and about $^1/_4$ inch apart at the bottom. Using the photograph on *page 145* as a guide, bend the end of the wire over the oval at the lower right side. Cut the end of the wire if necessary. Use the needlenose pliers to form the end of the wire into another tiny circle.
3. Cut a 6-inch piece of beading wire. Leaving a 1-inch tail, wrap the beading wire three times around the top of the oval loops. Starting with a silver bead, thread on all the beads, alternating the colored beads with the silver beads. You will end with a silver bead. Push the wire back into the row of beads from the bottom, starting with the colored bead above the last silver bead you threaded on the wire. Wrap the remaining beading wire around the top of the oval loops. Twist the beading wire ends together to secure.
4. Thread the length of silver ribbon through the top loop to hang.

metallic stars
(As shown on page 145)

What you need

Waxed paper
Crayola Model Magic clay
Rolling pin
Star cookie cutters in
   various sizes
Paper clips
Wire cutter
Acrylic paint in silver and gold
Paintbrush
Eyelets or small metallic studs
18-gauge wire
Silver or gold key chains or
   ankle chains

What to do

1. Tear off a square of waxed paper. Place a small ball of clay in the center. Cover with another square of waxed paper. Press flat with hand. Use a rolling pin to roll clay until it is about $^1/_4$ inch thick. Remove top layer of waxed paper.
2. Use cookie cutters to cut star shapes from clay. Remove the excess clay. Unfold a paper clip once (it will form an "S" shape). Cut paper clip in the center using a wire cutter.

continued on page 148

joyful ornaments

Push the ends of one U paper clip shape into the top of the ornament. Let star shapes dry.
3. Paint the back of the stars silver or gold as desired. Let the paint dry. Turn over and paint the sides and top. Let the paint dry.
4. To embellish stars, use your finger to press studs or eyelets into the clay stars where desired. To attach stars together, carefully push 18-gauge wire through the stars to be attached. Shape the wire as desired.
5. Thread key chain through the top paper clip loops to make hangers.

beribboned ornaments
(As shown on page 144)

What you need
Ball ornament
Purchased satin ribbon flowers
Hot-glue gun and hot glue
1- to 1½-inch-wide ribbon in various lengths

What to do
1. Glue the satin flowers directly to the ornament

top or to a ribbon bow.
2. Use hot glue to attach the ribbons and satin flowers to the ornament, *left*. Let dry.

snowflakes-all-around ornament
(As shown on page 146)

What you need
Newspapers
Light blue ball ornament
White glass paint
Fine liner paintbrush
Pencil with round-tip eraser

What to do
1. Cover work surface with newspapers. Using the photo *below* as a guide, paint a symmetrical snowflake. Start by painting a + in the size you want the snowflake. Then add a smaller x over the +.
2. Add in details, painting the same marks on all extensions of the snowflake. To add small dots, dip the handle end of a paintbrush in paint and dot on the surface. Let the paint dry.
3. To add large dots to the background, dip the eraser end of a pencil into paint and dot on the surface. Let the paint dry.

Sources
- Look for round glass ornaments in crafts, discount, home decor, and drugstores.
- Look for glass paints in art and crafts stores.
- Look for armature wire, usually used for sculpting, in art stores. Solder can be purchased in home improvement, discount, and hardware stores.
- Look for gold and silver beading wire in crafts and discount stores.
- You can find Crayola Model Magic clay in crafts, art, discount stores, and office supply stores.
- Purchase metal studs and eyelets in crafts, fabric, and discount stores.
- Purchase ribbon flowers in crafts, discount, and fabric stores.

Crafting tips
- To paint the words, such as "Joy," use a small round-tip paintbrush. To add the highlights, use a fine-pointed paintbrush.
- When creating an ornament using wire, like the one on page 145, try to plan your design before bending the wire. If you bend the wire too much or incorrectly, it may break.

- When using clay, smooth any wrinkles by applying a drop of hot water to the clay surface and smoothing with finger while the clay is wet.
- If adding ribbon to a project, use glue sparingly so it does not show through.
- To draw a symmetrical snowflake, draw a "+" and an overlapping "x" (this will form the snowflake center). Use a measuring tape or ruler to get the lines straight and equal.
- For certain surfaces, such as thin glass, a low-temp glue may be safer than hot glue.

Cost to make project
For joy-to-the-world ornament:
$2 per ornament
For beaded coil trim:
$3 per ornament
For metallic stars:
$1 per ornament
For beribboned ornament:
$2 per ornament
For snowflakes-all-around ornament:
$1.50 per ornament

Suggested selling price
For joy-to-the-world ornament:
$8 for one
For beaded coil trim:
$9 for one
For metallic stars:
$5 for one

For beribboned ornament
$5 for one
For snowflakes-all-around ornament
$6 for one

Time to make project
10 to 30 minutes per ornament, depending on technique and intricacy of details

Timesaving tips
- Make many ornaments at a time in assembly-line manner.
- For an ornament made with wire, draw the full-size ornament shape on a piece of paper as a guide for shaping the wire.
- To embellish ornaments with beads, you may be able to use dangly beaded earrings on earwires, using the earwires to secure the embellishments in place.
- For ornaments made with clay, roll out and use a whole package of clay at once. This will speed up the process as well as ensure the clay is used before it dries out.

TO SELL IT

- So the ornaments don't roll off your display table, set each one on a handful of shredded paper, in a glass goblet, or on artificial snow.
- Do not place a price sticker on the ornament as it may pull off the finish or the glass ball may break. Instead, tie a price tag on a string to the hanger.
- Wrap ornaments in tissue and place in a small box when purchased.
- To add festivity to your display, use miniature lights to highlight your creations.

- Because clay ornaments may remain slightly soft after drying, wrap them well to avoid impressions being made on the surface.
- To add height to your display, hang ornaments on a tabletop tree, artificial large tree, or a feather tree.
- Display other uses for ornaments, such as gift trims, wreath embellishments, or possible napkin ring holders or centerpiece trims.
- Save all of the original packaging when purchasing holiday ornaments. These come in handy for storing, transporting, and packaging.

- When selling glass or other fragile ornaments, have bubble wrap on hand for safe packing.
- To make a hanger that is quick and inexpensive, tie curling ribbon to the top of the ornament.
- Provide a savings when customers purchase six or more ornaments.
- Egg cartons work well for storing small ornaments.
- When selling at crafts shows other than the Christmas season, make ornaments for Easter, Halloween, the Fourth of July, and Valentine's Day.

TO GIVE IT

- When appropriate, personalize an ornament by painting the recipient's name on the front.
- Coordinate the colors of the ornament, paint, and ribbons, etc. to match the decor of someone special.
- Tie a small sprig of evergreen to the top of a wrapped gift, adding your handcrafted ornament.
- For a great hostess gift, tie an ornament around the neck of a bottle of champagne, sparkling cider, or hot chocolate mix.

- Place an ornament in a small basket, filled with holiday greens and tied with coordinating ribbon.
- For a fun mailing container, use a quart paint can (available in paint stores) and pack well with shredded paper or bubble wrap.
- For someone with limited space, make miniature ornaments and place on a tabletop tree.
- When appropriate, use a permanent marking pen to record the year and your signature.

- For an extra-special presentation, give a different ornament during each of the 12 days of Christmas.
- To be one of Santa's helpers, tie an ornament to the hanger of each Christmas stocking.
- For a clever gift wrap, purchase a holiday stocking just large enough to hold the ornament.
- To make a little more of your gift, add a pair of plain coordinating ball ornaments with your handcrafted trim.

sweet caroling cherubs

Singing the joys of the season, these adorable angels add heavenly touches throughout the home. Gracing the tree, a banister, or tied to a centerpiece, they can be displayed separately or as a choir.

What you need

1-inch wood ball with drilled holes
10-inch-long dowel to fit into ball
Thick white crafts glue
Acrylic paints in golden brown, peach, brown, and gold
Small flat or round paintbrush
Small stencil brush
Very fine liner brush
Clear sealer
Yarn
10-inch-long piece of 2-inch-wide gold wired ribbon
Thread
Hot-glue gun and hot glue
Satin flower
⅛-inch-wide ribbon

What to do

1. Insert the dowel into the wood ball. Glue into place and let dry.
2. Paint the wooden ball with the desired flesh color. Let it dry. Paint a round gold cap on head. Let it dry. To paint cheeks, use the stencil brush and very little peach paint.
3. Using a fine liner brush, paint eyes using brown paint. Using the photograph as a guide, paint two half-moon shapes and eyelashes. Paint a small brown oval for mouth. Let dry. Paint wood head with sealer.
4. Run a line of thick white crafts glue along edge of dowel. Pull one end out from a skein of yarn and tie tightly below the head. Wind yarn around the entire dowel, keeping the wraps smooth and even. Continue winding around the dowel to make the body shape wide at the top and narrow at the bottom.
5. To make gold wings, fold the ends of the gold wired ribbon in toward the center overlapping at least 1 inch in the middle. With thread, wind and tie very tightly around the center to hold it together and make a bow shape. Hot-glue it to the back of the angel right below the head.
6. Apply hot glue to the flower and place it on the front of the angel, right below the chin.
7. Make a small ribbon loop and hot glue it to the back for hanging.

Sources

- Wooden heads usually come in a package with several balls of the same size. Purchase them in crafts and discount stores in the wood crafts section. For this project you should get the balls that have a flat side and a predrilled hole.

Crafting tips

- To paint the fine details, it is important to use a good quality fine liner brush, such as a size 0 or 00. You may spend up to $10 for one, but it will make a very big difference. The inexpensive fine brushes cannot achieve the same results.
- When painting fine details like the eyelashes, thin the

paint and use very little. The paint should not well up at the tip of the brush. If it does, you have too much paint.

Cost to make project
$2 per cherub

Suggested selling price
$8 for one, $21 for three

Time to make project
1 hour

Timesaving tip

- To speed up painting the caps on the heads, you can use gold spray paint. From a 4-inch piece of heavy card stock, cut out a circle the exact size of the golden cap. It has to fit snugly over the ball. Place it on the ball to expose where you want the cap and spray with paint.

TO SELL IT

- Make cherubs with a variety of skin tones.
- For teachers, have the angel hold an apple instead of a flower.

TO GIVE IT

- Attach a cherub to the bow of a wrapped gift for an extra holiday touch.
- Personalize angels by selecting various charms or miniature items (found by the doll accessories in crafts stores) for the angels to hold.

coiled christmas trees

Add sparkle to any tabletop with these metallic trees dripping in jewels. Topped with a brilliant star, these jolly trees are stunning when grouped together in various sizes.

What you need
Bottle with narrow neck
Armature wire approximately
  45 inches long
Tracing paper
Pencil
38-gauge gold and silver
  aluminum
Wire cutters
Scissors
Hot-glue gun and hot glue
Rhinestones and gems

What to do
1. Find a bottle with a narrow neck that tapers to a wider bottom. It should have a cone shape to coil around. Some soft drink bottles will work. Also some catsup, salad dressing, and wine bottles work well. Holding the bottle firmly, wrap the wire around the bottle, beginning on the top and winding downward. Keep the wire taut, and each revolution around the bottle should be wound tightly against the next.
2. When the piece of wire is completely wound, remove from bottle, lifting upward off the narrow end. Adjust the coil to desired shape, pulling apart to increase height and widen or narrow coils to desired shape. Experiment with different bottles and a variety of wire lengths to create trees tall and thin, short and plump, leaning or perfectly straight. Point the top end of the wire upward to hold the star.
3. Trace the star patterns, *right*. Trace star shapes onto aluminum using a sharp pointed pencil. Cut out star shapes from aluminum using scissors. Cut tiny slits on the inside points of the large star.
4. Lay the small star centered on top of the large star. Fold in the edges of the back star over to the front star. Leave an opening and slip onto the top of the tree. Use a spot of hot glue to hold in place.
5. Add gems to the tree by placing small random dots of hot glue on the wire. Immediately put the gems on the glue. Place one at the bottom end of the coil and add gems to each point of the star.

Sources
- Purchase armature wire in hobby, crafts stores, and art stores. It is often used for sculpture.
- Purchase soft 38-gauge aluminum (decorator foil) in art and crafts stores.

Crafting tip
- Protect your work surface when using hot glue.

Cost to make project
$3.50 per tree

Suggested selling price
$9 each or three for $24

Time to make project
½ hour

Timesaving tips
- Make several trees in stages—coil, make stars, glue on gems.
- Cut more than one metal star shape at a time by layering two or three pieces of metal before cutting.

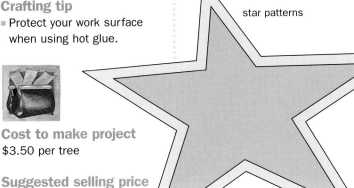

star patterns

TO SELL IT
- Place trees out of the reach of children, so they aren't tempted to pull on the wires.
- On your selling table, place in groups of three, making one very tall. Coordinate the gem colors for a grouping.

TO GIVE IT
- These small trees make a big hit when display space is limited. Give these trees to people in nursing homes or in the hospital.
- If you plan to mail a coiled tree, place it over a cone-shape bottle or piece of foam to help maintain its shape.

jolly paper tags

Keep tags close at hand to send a personal note or to make sure a gift reaches the right person. These lovely examples use scraps from other paper projects. To create the shapes, use our samples as a guide to make your patterns—or trace around objects you have at home.

What you need

Cookie cutters, cups, boxes, or other shapes to trace
Pencil
Scraps of decorative art papers
Decorative-edge and regular scissors
Glue stick
Paper punch the approximate size of eyelet
Eyelets and eyelet tool
Buttons
Thick white crafts glue
Thin cording

What to do

1. Decide what shape you wish to make your tag. Look at the photograph, *opposite*, for inspiration or create your own shapes by tracing around items such as cookie cutters, cups, and boxes. The tag can be one-sided, or it can fold.

2. Trace around the desired shape onto the background paper. Cut out the shape. As shown, you can layer papers by cutting the top layer slightly smaller than the bottom layer.
3. Cut additional trim pieces, such as stripes or leaves, from art papers using decorative-edge or regular scissors. Glue the pieces in place using a glue stick.
4. To add eyelets to the design or to make a reinforced hole for the cording, use a paper punch to make a hole. Then slip in an eyelet and use the eyelet tool to secure it in place.
5. If desired, arrange a single button or a group of buttons on the front of the tag. Glue the buttons in place using thick white crafts glue. Let the glue dry.
6. If desired, thread a piece of cording through the top eyelet to attach to a gift.

Sources

- Purchase decorative-edge scissors in crafts, art, and discount stores.
- Look for art papers in art supply stores.

Crafting tips

- When not in use, keep art papers from creasing by rolling them around an empty wrapping paper tube.
- If you do not have thick white crafts glue on hand, you can carefully sew on the button trims using a needle and thread or two plies of embroidery floss.
- Some decorative-edge scissors tend to tear art papers. To get a cleaner cut, sandwich the art paper between two pieces of typing paper when cutting.

Cost to make project
10¢ to 50¢ per tag

Suggested selling price
$1 for one, $5 for six

Time to make project
10 minutes

Timesaving tips

- Layer papers before cutting and cut out several shapes at once.
- Make several tags in stages: Trace, cut, embellish, etc.
- If eyelets are purchased with several colors in a package, separate colors and place in sandwich bags.
- To glue small pieces of paper, use a toothpick to take a small dab from the glue stick.

TO SELL IT

- Bundle 6 to 10 tags and tie with a bow to sell as a set.
- Make some tags without cords and sell them with envelopes to use as greeting cards.

TO GIVE IT

- Make these clever tags in a variety of colors and give them as a gift for others to use year-round.
- To use as a gift tag on a large package, thread ribbon through eyelet instead of cording.

FLORAL
AND
NATURE

Everyone loves to be surrounded by the beauty of nature.

From front-door wreaths to tabletop topiaries,

potpourri boxes to shimmering basil pots, you'll be inspired

with this chapter's variety of projects that bring the

great outdoors in. The next time you go on a walk, take

along a pail to gather materials for nature crafting.

A WALK WITH NATURE

Making Projects with Natural Materials

One of the most enjoyable steps in making crafts with natural materials is finding the materials! While crafts and discount stores carry natural supplies for crafting, such as dried flowers, leaves, rocks, and grapevines, finding items like these during a walk is fun and doesn't cost a thing.

Always keep a pail or plastic bags with handles in the car, in the back of a stroller, or tied to your bike. Then when you are enjoying the great outdoors, keep your eyes open for twigs, leaves, acorns, pinecones, fallen bark pieces, shells, and more.

When you return home, wash the items thoroughly and let them dry. Sort the items into containers so you can find exactly what you need while crafting.

When collecting flowers for pressing, place them flat between sheets of waxed paper and tuck them in the middle of a heavy book. To dry floral finds, secure stems together with a wire twist or a rubber band and hang upside down in a cool, dark place until dry.

Selling Floral and Nature Items

Items made with natural materials are often fragile. Be sure to have packaging materials ready, such as tissue paper and bubble wrap. To transport some items, a strong bag with handles may be the answer. Whatever you choose, be sure your projects will be well protected while your customers continue to shop.

If you have the space in your booth or under your selling table, you may want to offer a place to hold purchased items for customers until they leave. Be sure to mark the item "sold," keep a record of the customer's name, collect the money for the sale, and give the customer a receipt indicating the exact item purchased.

When pricing floral and nature crafts, be creative with the tags. A leaf or a torn piece of art paper makes tags that have the same natural look as the crafts themselves. This adds perceived value and showcases your creativity. If you specialize in floral and nature crafts, choose a design for your business card that complements this talent.

If you're selling wreaths, keep extra ribbon on hand. You can change this final embellishment to suit a customer's tastes if desired. If you wish to offer this option, display the ribbons and widths that are available.

Offer tips on cleaning and storing all of the items you sell. It also may be interesting to include a short description of the unusual materials used in the project. The topiaries on *page 172* are a good example.

pretty basil pots

Garden herbs of any sort are right at home in these glimmering pots decorated with painted clay leaves. Sell these stunning pots with plants, or let your customers pot their own favorite herbs.

What you need
Waxed paper
Red bakeable clay, such as Ovencraft
Rolling pin
Tiny leaf cookie cutter about 1 inch long
4-inch terra-cotta pot with saucer
Knife
Cookie sheet
Acrylic paints in metallic copper, green, purple, and blue
Paintbrush
Foam plate
Natural painting sponge
Waterproof adhesive, such as Liquid Nails

continued on page 162

Container herbs
Many herbs grow well in containers, both indoors and out, making it possible for people without gardening space to grow herbs and to extend the growing season for tender herbs in cold climates. Herbs that grow well in containers:

Basil	Marjoram
Bay	Mint
Borage	Mint marigold
Catmint	
Catnip	Parsley
Chervil	Rosemary
Chives	Sage
Greek oregano	Savory
	Scented geraniums
Hyssop	
Lavender	Sorrel
Lemon balm	Tarragon
	Thyme

Sources
- Purchase red clay in crafts, art, and hobby stores.
- Look for tiny cookie cutters with clay accessories in crafts and art stores or in specialty cooking stores.

Floral tips
- Use any color of acrylic paint. The colors may fade if kept outside long term. You can also use paint designated for outdoor use.
- Be sure to keep your sponge clean while working. Don't over-blend the paint; just blend it enough to create several colors.
- Copy leaf shapes or other items from nature for clay pot trims.

TO SELL IT
- Fill pots with potting soil and plant herb seeds 6 to 8 weeks before sale date.
- Fresh leaves, ferns, even grasses make great tablecloths on which to display your pots.

TO GIVE IT
- Place a basil plant into the pot before gift-giving, along with the growing and transplanting instructions.
- Fill the pot with basil seeds for planting, along with favorite recipes using the herb.

Cost to make project
$2 per pot with plant

Suggested selling price
$6 to $18, depending on size of pot

Time to make project
2 hours

Timesaving tip
- It is more efficient to mass-produce these rather than one at a time. Make all the leaves at one time, bake them at another time, and line up many pots and paint all the same color combinations. Paint different color combinations at another time. When pots are finished, fill them in a large area where they can remain undisturbed for several weeks.

pretty basil pots

What to do

▲ **1.** Place a piece of waxed paper on work surface. On waxed paper, roll out clay to about ³⁄₁₆ inch thick. Use a cookie cutter to cut out leaf shapes. (You can cut out shape with a sharp knife if you do not have a cookie cutter.)

▲ **2.** Carefully pick up leaf shapes and press onto the pot, gently shaping to the curve of the pot. While leaf is on the pot, press in lines for detail using a knife. Carefully remove the leaf shapes from the pot and gently lay onto cookie sheet, maintaining the leaf shape so it will fit the pot later. Let the clay dry at least one day, until it does not feel cool.

3. Bake the clay leaves in the oven according to instructions on clay label. Let the leaf shapes cool before handling.

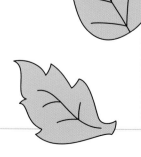

leaf patterns

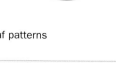

◀ **4.** Paint the leaves green and the saucer a solid color, such as metallic green or copper. Let the paint dry.

◀ **5.** To paint the pots, place the desired colors of paint on a foam plate. Soak sponge in water and squeeze out excess. Dip sponge in paint and dab onto the pot surface. Alternate with different colors, rinsing paint from sponge each time you change colors. Dab the clean sponge onto the wet paint until the colors are blended. Let the paint dry.

▲ **6.** Place a small dab of adhesive onto the back side of the leaves and glue onto the painted pot as desired.

leaves-aplenty wreath

Full of texture and subtle color, these circular wreaths boast lovely collections from the sea, the woods, and the garden. A ribbon or raffia bow adds a perfect crowning touch. The instructions begin on page 168.

by-the-seashore wreath

across-the-land wreaths

wreaths in a row

across-the-land wreaths

leaves-aplenty wreath
(As shown on page 164)

What you need
Purchased glycerine-preserved leaves
Newspaper
Optional floral paint spray in red, purple, and yellow
9-inch straw circular wreath
Thick white crafts glue
T-pins
Natural raffia
Gold spray paint
Plastic grapes

What to do
1. If you wish to enhance or intensify the color of the leaves, you can apply floral paint in a well-ventilated area. Spread out the leaves on newspaper and spray spots of color using a random motion. Spray only edges and small portions of leaves. Spray the purple very lightly over the red. Overlay the yellow onto the red. Let the leaves dry.
2. Coat the wreath well with glue. Beginning at the bottom of the wreath, arrange leaves onto wreath base overlapping each other. Pin the leaves in place as you go. Insert the pin in an inconspicuous place, such as near the stem. When the leaves begin to set firmly into the glue, you may remove the pins. Let the glue dry.

3. Cut a small bundle of raffia approximately 36 inches long. Lay the raffia on newspaper and spread apart. Spray with gold spray paint. Let the paint dry. Turn the raffia over and spray again. Let dry.
4. Tie the painted raffia into a bow and glue onto the top of the wreath. Pin the bow in place, hiding the pin in the raffia. Trim the tails of the raffia as desired.
5. Pin the cluster of grapes underneath the bow.

by-the-seashore wreath
(As shown on page 165)

What you need
10-inch round plastic foam wreath form, such as Styrofoam
Low-temp glue gun and hot-glue sticks
Thick jute rope; scissors
2 yards of 1½-inch-wide peach-colored ribbon
1½ yards of ivory cord
Seashells
Gold shell charms

What to do
1. To cover the round wreath form with jute rope, put a dab of glue on the back of the wreath. Press the end of the rope into the glue. Let the glue set up. Wrap the rope around the wreath, keeping the rope close together and gluing about every inch on the back side. Continue wrapping until the entire shape is covered. Clip the rope and glue the end to the back of the form. Let the glue dry.
2. Wrap the rope-covered wreath form with ribbon, tying the ends into a bow. Loosely wrap the wreath with cord, knotting the ends together near the bow.
3. Decide on the placement of the shells, tucking some under the cord and adding one to the center of the ribbon bow. Use glue to secure shells in place. Glue charms to the cord ends and wherever else you wish to add them. Let the glue dry.

wreaths in a row
(As shown on pages 166–167)

What you need
Hot-glue gun and hot-glue sticks
Three 3-inch grapevine wreaths
Small dried flowers in three coordinating colors
18-inch-long bundle of sticks
1-inch-wide sheer ribbon
Fine wire, if needed
Rose bud heads

What to do
1. Use hot glue to attach dried flowers to the wreaths. Cover two, using the same color of flowers. The other two flower colors will be used for the remaining wreath and in the center of the sticks, as shown in the photograph on *pages 166–167*. Cover one side of each wreath completely. Let dry.
2. If the sticks are not tied together, secure by winding the center with wire.
3. Thread 24-inch-long pieces of ribbon through each of the wreath shapes. Tie the matching wreaths on each end of the stick bundle, letting each hang 1 inch below sticks. Slip the ribbon ends to the top of the sticks. Tie the remaining wreath in the center, letting it dangle 3 inches from sticks. Slip the ribbon ends to the top of the wreath. Tie the ribbon ends into bows.
4. Using the photograph as a guide, glue a few of the remaining color of small flowers to the center of the stick bundle. Make the arrangement about 7 inches wide. Fill in with rose bud heads. Let the glue dry.

Sources

- Purchase dried flowers and rosebud heads in crafts stores and discount stores, or you can dry them from your garden.
- Look for grapevine and straw wreath forms in a variety of sizes in crafts and discount stores.
- Purchase glycerine-preserved leaves in the floral department of crafts and discount stores.
- Purchase plastic grapes in crafts and discount stores, and gift shops.
- Look for inexpensive seashells in crafts stores and gift shops, or you can pick them up on a walk along the seashore.
- Purchase plastic foam wreath forms, such as Styrofoam, in a variety of sizes in crafts and discount stores.

Floral tips

Leaves-aplenty wreath:
- Practice spray painting on paper first to experiment with overlaying different colors. Try different colors, such as overlaying green onto red and green onto yellow and adding purple onto red, green, or yellow.

- Spray-paint lightly and keep your hand moving. Do not stop or you will get a too-heavy coat or excessive paint that will run or puddle.
- Use a low-temp glue gun on Styrofoam as it doesn't melt the surface like a hot-glue gun.

Wreaths in a row:
- Be very careful when using a hot-glue gun. It can burn fingers as well as the work surface.

Cost to make project

Leaves-aplenty wreath:
Approximately $8
By-the-seashore wreath:
$3–$5 per wreath, depending on size and materials used
Wreaths in a row:
$3 per trio

Suggested selling price

Leaves-aplenty wreath:
$15–$20, depending on size
By-the-seashore wreath:
$8–$18, depending on size
Wreaths in a row:
$18

Time to make project

Leaves-aplenty wreath:
1½ hours
By-the-seashore wreath:
½ hour
Wreaths in a row:
45 minutes

TO SELL IT

- Make wreaths using a variety of color combinations.
- Display wreaths hung on pegboard for ease in setting up and for customer accessibility.
- Display wreaths propped on wooden crates, old doors, or distressed shutters.

- Wrap purchased wreaths in bubble wrap to protect the leaves from breakage.
- Display as wall or door wreaths, candle rings, and shelf decor items.
- Make wreaths in a variety of sizes using various bow and trim colors.
- Use flea-market finds, such as spoons, bottles, and jewelry, to embellish wreaths.

TO GIVE IT

- Create a wreath trio in colors that coordinate with a friend's or relative's home.
- Wreaths make great anniversary gifts and can be made using the original wedding flower colors.
- Give a wreath as a hostess gift at Thanksgiving.
- Instead of using grapes, personalize a wreath with a gold-painted wooden initial.

- Purchase a sea-themed postcard to use as a coordinating gift tag for the by-the-seashore wreath.
- To make into a mirror, use a strong adhesive to glue a round mirror to the wreath form after it is wound with rope, ribbon, and cording.
- A purchased hatbox makes a great presentation as well as a storage box.

Time-saving tips

Leaves-aplenty wreath:
- Do several at a time, laying out a large area of leaves and a large bundle of raffia to spray-paint.

By-the-seashore wreath:
- Wrap several wreath shapes with rope, ribbon, and cording—then have fun adding the shells, charms, and other desired embellishments.

Wreaths in a row:
- Cut dried flowers with a scissors, cutting 1 to 1½-inch lengths.

a-stroll-in-the-woods box

This artistic box looks expensive, but the supplies cost little or nothing at all. Adaptable to any size or shape of box, you can make each work of art a one-of-a-kind.

What you need
Papier mâché box with lid
Pencil
Leaves, acorns, evergreen, pinecones, and weeds
White glue
White gesso
Sand
Acrylic paints in pumpkin and black; paintbrush
Acrylic sealer
Soft rag
Rub 'n Buff gold

What to do
1. Place the lid onto the box and draw a pencil line on the box around the bottom of the lid. This will indicate where the lid fits onto the box so that area is not covered with dimensional items.
2. Decide how you would like to arrange the nature items on the box. Glue pieces into place using white glue. Let the glue dry.
3. Paint the entire box with a coat of white

gesso to give it all an even color and strengthen any weak items, such as leaves. Sprinkle a little sand in wet gesso for added texture. Let it dry.
4. Paint the entire piece with pumpkin-colored paint. Let it dry.
5. Paint the entire piece with clear sealer. Let it dry. Apply a second coat of sealer. Let it dry.
6. Thin a small amount of black acrylic paint with water so that it is very thin. Paint onto entire textured surface, especially filling in the deep crevices. Dab off the excess paint before it dries, leaving dark paint in the crevices. Let dry.
7. Highlight the raised areas with gold Rub 'n Buff. Place a small amount on fingertip and very lightly rub over most raised areas. This may take some practice to avoid overdoing it.

Sources
- You can find many nature items right in your own backyard or on a walk in the woods. Use anything that will hold a nice shape when painted over.
- Papier mâché boxes are available in a variety of sizes and shapes in crafts and discount stores. You can also use any sturdy cardboard box with a lid, such as those from oatmeal, bank checks, or jewelry.

Floral tip
- Use a good-size, fairly coarse brush to paint effectively and quickly on the rough areas.

TO SELL IT
- Surround nature boxes with pinecones, leaves, and other nature finds.
- Suggest uses for boxes, such as enclosing a bagged loaf of bread, potpourri made from nature items, or bath beads.

TO GIVE IT
- Trim small boxes using this same method and enclose small gifts, such as a deck of cards, jewelry, or a CD.
- Make a gift tag from a leaf or fern, writing on it with permanent marker or paint pen.

Cost to make project
$3

Suggested selling price
$8 to $24, depending on box size and intricacy of design

Time to make project
2½ hours

Timesaving tips
- Make several boxes in stages.
- Ask the kids to go on a hunt for nature items to decorate the boxes.
- Using small boxes, decorate the center of the lid only.
- If using acorns as a trim, ask someone to check all of the caps. If any are loose, glue them in place. Let the glue dry before using.

blooming topiaries

Unusual items from nature combine to make striking tabletop topiaries. You can dry your own flowers and weeds or purchase favorite varieties from a crafts or discount store. Include a topiary in an arrangement of decorative items or line up three or four along a windowsill or mantel for an eye-catching display.

What you need
Bell cups
Vine-wrapped bamboo
Garden clippers
Hot-glue gun and hot glue
Plastic foam pieces, such
  as Styrofoam
Small terra-cotta pots
Sharpened pencil
Dried flowers, pods, and leaves
Small rocks

What to do
1. Pull the wire stem from the bell cup. Cut a length of bamboo, 8 inches long for a small topiary, 10 inches long for a large topiary. Glue the bamboo length to the bottom of the bell cup (attach a small bell cup to the 8-inch length or a large bell cup to the 10-inch length). Let the glue dry.
2. Wedge a small piece of plastic foam into the terra-cotta pot, leaving 1 inch at the top. Push a

sharpened pencil down in the center of the plastic foam. Remove the pencil. Fill the hole in the plastic foam halfway with glue. Push the end of the bamboo into the glue as far as possible, being careful not to disturb the bell cup. Straighten the bamboo and hold it for a few seconds until the glue begins to set. Let the glue dry.
3. Cut a small piece of plastic foam to fit into the bell cup. Glue in place.
4. Decide how you want to arrange the dried nature items in the bell cup. Press the stems into the plastic foam, gluing as necessary. Add dried items to the bamboo stem and near the base as desired.
5. Fill the terra-cotta pot with rocks to hide the plastic foam and to add weight to the base.

Sources
- Purchase the bell cups, bamboo, and dried nature items in the artificial floral section of crafts or discount stores.

Floral tips
- To make sure the plastic foam pieces stay in place, use dots of glue to secure.
- There are many types of dried flowers, leaves, and pods available. While some are rather expensive, some are sold in large bunches at a more reasonable price.
- You can dry items from your garden. For a particular variety, research the best drying method. Two common methods are using silica sand and hanging the items upside down in a cool, dark place.

Cost to make project
$6

Suggested selling price
$11 for the small topiary,
$16 for the large topiary

Time to make project
1 hour

Timesaving tips
- Make several topiaries in stages.
- Remove the wire stems for the bell cups using pliers.
- If the terra-cotta pots have sticky spots left from the original price tags, remove the residue with a purchased cleaner created for this purpose.
- Keep materials organized in separate containers to make assembly quick.
- Discard any leaves or other materials that are broken or unusable.

TO SELL IT
- Make coordinating sets to encourage multiple sales.
- On the price tag, list the types of dried flowers and other materials used in the top of the topiary.

TO GIVE IT
- Made from dried materials, these topiaries make everlasting gifts.
- If giving a topiary in person, no wrap is needed. Just tie a ribbon around the stem.

dainty potpourri box

This beautiful box, holding fresh floral scents, is accented with painted clay shapes. A gel stain is applied as the last coat to add a whitewashed effect. Fill to the brim with an aromatic potpourri to make this dainty box irresistible.

What you need
Crayola Model Magic clay
Rolling pin
Small heart cookie cutter
Butter knife
Thick white crafts glue
Round box with lid
  approximately 6 inches in
  diameter and 3½ inches
  high
Acrylic paints in white, red,
  green, pale and bright
  yellow, and blue
Fine point and small flat
  paintbrushes
White gel stain
Damp, soft cloth

What to do
1. Roll out clay to a thickness of approximately ³⁄₁₆ inch. Cut out 4 small hearts with cookie cutter. Set aside to dry.
2. Shape leaves by forming a marble-size ball out of clay. Flatten it into an oval shape, and press a crease into the center with the blade of a knife.
3. Form 7 or 8 small balls to place in the center of the flower. To make the blue flowers around the edge, form 5 balls of clay for each flower. Shape tiny leaves out of clay. Let shapes dry.
4. Glue clay shapes onto the lid and sides of the box.

continued on page 176

Sources
- Purchase boxes in a variety of shapes and sizes in discount and crafts stores.
- Look for Crayola Model Magic in crafts, art, discount, and some office supply stores.

Floral tip
- You can save money by drying your own flowers to make potpourri. Dry them in silica sand following the directions on the sand product, or use naturally dried straw flowers. Place them in an airtight plastic bag with 3 or 4 drops of scented oil, shake very gently, and leave overnight.

Cost to make project
$4, excluding cost for potpourri

Suggested selling price
$16, including potpourri

Time to make project
2 hours

Timesaving tips
- Use cotton cording instead of making clay ropes.
- Use naturally scented dried flowers, such as lavender, to make the potpourri.
- Cut out several clay shapes and roll several tiny balls before beginning to assemble the pieces on the lid.
- Instead of using the variety of clay shapes shown, choose one large cookie cutter shape to place in the center of the lid. Keep the details to a minimum.

TO SELL IT
- Make sets of three, using box sizes that nest together.
- Sell some boxes and potpourri mixes separately.
- Paint the boxes using a variety of color combinations.

TO GIVE IT
- These boxes make perfect gifts for moms, teachers, aunts, and grandmothers.
- Decorate the box with a Christmas motif, such as holly leaves and berries or a single poinsettia. Fill the box with holiday potpourri to give and display at Christmas.

▲ **5.** Coil a piece of clay into a ⅛-inch-thick rope to trim the edge of lid. Place a thin line of glue around the edge and add the rope of clay around the edge, meeting at each flower. Let the clay dry on the box.

▲ **6.** Paint the entire box, inside and out, using white. Let the paint dry. Paint the box pale yellow. Slightly overlap the paint onto the flowers and rope. Let the paint dry. Paint the large flowers red, the leaves and rope green, the small flowers blue, and all the flower centers bright yellow. Let the paint dry.

▲ 7. Coat the entire outside of the box and the lid using a generous amount of white gel stain. Brush the gel stain into all of the crevices of the clay design.

▲ 8. Let the gel just begin to dry and gently wipe off with the damp, soft cloth. Don't overwipe; just wipe enough to take the top surface off, leaving the white stain in the crevices. Let the stain dry.

9. Fill the box with your choice of purchased or homemade potpourri.

nutty bugs

These silly characters will love poking around houseplants. Made from two easy-to-find supplies—nuts and wire—you can create an entire troop of these bugs in no time.

What you need for the bugs or worm

English walnuts, pecans, hickory nuts, and acorns
Saw
Hot-glue gun and hot-glue sticks
Drill and a 3/32-inch bit
Wirecutters
18-gauge black wire
Needlenose pliers

bugs

What to do
1. Saw a nut in half lengthwise. Clean out the inside of the shell. Fill the shell with glue and let cool.
2. Drill two holes near one end of the shell for antennae. Drill two more holes near the center of the body, for bugs with wings.
3. Cut enough 2-inch-long pieces of wire to make the legs and antennae. Use pliers to make a loop at the end of each wire to make feet or antennae ends. Trim the pieces to the desired length.
4. Use pliers to push the legs into place in the dried glue. Insert the antennae into the holes in the shell. Bend an 8- to 10-inch piece of wire to form the shape of the wings, so the ends of the wire end up together near the other two holes in the shell. Insert the wings into the holes in the shell.

acorn worm

What to do
1. Remove the caps from the acorns. Drill two holes completely through the sides of four acorns. On a fifth acorn, drill one hole in the side and two holes near the top on the opposite side for the antennae.
2. Cut a 10-inch piece of wire and fold it in half. Insert the ends through the two holes in the first acorn and pull the acorn onto the wire as far as possible. Repeat with the three remaining acorn pieces.
3. Push the ends of the wires through the side hole in the last acorn. Push a wire through each top hole. Pull the acorn tightly against the others.
4. Trim the wire ends to the desired length of the antennae. Use pliers to make a loop in the end of each wire to look like antennae.

Sources
- Find nuts under appropriate trees or purchase them in a grocery store.
- Purchase wire and needlenose pliers in home centers and crafts stores.

Floral tips
- You do not have to wait for the glue to be completely set before adding wires. Do be careful not to handle too early, however, as hot glue can cause serious burns.
- To give these creatures even more personality, you can paint the bodies using acrylic paint. To paint the wire pieces, poke the ends into a block of plastic foam to act as a holder while painting. Spray wires with paint suitable for metal.

Cost to make project
25¢ per bug

Suggested selling price
$1.50 for one bug, six for $8

Time to make project
30 minutes per bug

Timesaving tips
- Cut and shape several wire pieces before beginning to assemble bugs.
- Drill all of the holes for the bugs at one time.
- Use thin lead-free solder for the wire details. This is soft enough to bend by hand.
- While working on bugs, keep the nuts in a pie tin to prevent them from rolling off the work surface.
- Use small plastic containers to organize the different wire pieces.

TO SELL IT
- Sell the plant pokes separately or in sets.
- Set up a fun display by incorporating props from nature—stumps, twigs, leaves, pinecones, etc.

TO GIVE IT
- Place a bug plant poke in a potted plant. For someone ill, attach a tag that reads, "Heard you have a bug."
- Make lapel pins in the same manner by adding a piece of cardboard and a pin to the back of the nut.

colorful nature finds

Pinecones and acorns exhibit a natural beauty in their texture and shape. Enhanced with metallic paints, these from-the-ground finds get a real pick-me-up. You may be able to find these items in your part of the country, or you can purchase them in a crafts store. Explore which pods or other natural items are suitable for this colorful autumn project.

What you need

Acorns
Pinecones
Paper towels
Newspapers
Acrylic metallic paints in desired colors
Disposable foam plate
Paintbrush
Small sponge paintbrush
Thick white crafts glue

What to do

1. If necessary, rinse acorns and pinecones under water to remove any dirt or dust. Place them on paper towels to dry.
2. Cover your work surface with newspapers. Place a small amount of each metallic paint color on a disposable foam plate, leaving space between the colors.

3. Paint the pinecones a solid color. To paint the crevices of the pinecones, use an old or small sponge paintbrush and gently poke it into the areas where paint is needed. If desired, you can leave some of the natural pinecone color show and only paint the outer tips. Let the paint dry.
4. Check the tops on the acorns to be sure they are secure. If loose, glue the tops back on using thick white crafts glue. Let the glue dry.
5. Paint the acorn bottoms a solid color. Let the paint dry. Paint the tops a contrasting color. Let the paint dry.

Sources
- Look for acrylic metallic paints in art, crafts, and discount stores.

Floral tips
- To avoid ruining a new paintbrush, be sure to use an old brush or small sponge brush when painting pinecones. You can push the paintbrush bristles or the tip of the sponge brush into the pinecone crevices.
- Use non-metallic paints in autumn colors to create another interesting look on acorns and pinecones.
- Add tiny dots to the bottoms of the acorns by using a toothpick or the end of paintbrush handle dipped in paint.

Cost to make project
5¢ per item

Suggested selling price
50¢ each

Time to make project
2 to 5 minutes per item

Timesaving tips
- Use light coats of metallic spray paint instead of painting with a brush.
- Paint one-half of the item and let it dry. Then you'll have something to hold onto when finishing the paint job.
- If using a spray-paint method, you may want to drill small holes in the items first. Insert a wire and poke the other end into a block of plastic foam. This will act as a holder so you can paint the entire item at once.

TO SELL IT

- To keep items from rolling, place painted acorns and pinecones in baskets, bowls, candleholders, cornucopias, or on top of greenery or sticks.

TO GIVE IT

- Mix painted acorns and pinecones in with purchased potpourri.
- Arrange a collection of pinecones and acorns in a wooden bowl.

FLEA
MARKET
TRANSFORMATIONS

Welcome to a world where the old, worn,

and discarded are given new life. You'll find yourself

on a treasure hunt the next time you're at a flea market,

thrift shop, or garage sale—in search of the

just-right finds to re-create these best-selling projects.

All it takes is a keen eye and a creative hand to complete

these clever transformations.

WHAT A FIND

Making Projects with Flea Market Items

A great outlet for expressing creativity is to discover new uses for castaway items. Once you've been challenged with the fun crafts in this chapter, you'll be inspired to experiment with other flea market finds to combine with your crafting talents.

Flea markets, garage sales, antiques stores, estate auctions, secondhand shops, and charity organizations are good places to start your hunt for crafting materials. Keep an open mind as you stroll through each aisle. Could you make a lampshade from a vintage china bowl?

How could you give a dented watering can new life? What can you do with mismatched silverware?

When you find an interesting item, don't purchase it unless you have a plan for how to use it. Make a note of where you saw the item and the price. If you come up with a way to use it in your crafting, return soon to the shop to purchase the item. Otherwise, you may end up with a garage full of junk for a garage sale and no crafting supplies.

When at an auction, keep your budget in mind. It's easy to get caught up in the excitement and lose track of your goals.

Although you may have a great use for something you see, it may not be a reasonable price for you, as a crafter, to pay. Remember, when selling crafts, profit is the name of the game.

Selling Crafts Made from Flea Market Finds

If any of your flea-market finds have a history, be sure to record this for customers on a label or tag. Shoppers may be interested to know that the Christmas ornaments they're holding were once stairway spindles. Or that the adorable birdhouses are made from vintage rolling pins. Or that chair you've painted is from the late 1800s. Fun facts like these add interest to these one-of-a-kind crafts.

When buying flea-market items for crafting, be sure to record the price paid for each piece and where it was purchased. Whatever kind of crafting you do, be sure to take your expenses and time investment into consideration when pricing your items.

You won't need to purchase any price tags if you're crafting with flea-market finds. Use your imagination and recycle items to create tags. Tear small pieces from used envelopes, cut fabric swatches, or write on large buttons or small metal washers. Think of clever ways to coordinate tags with your handcrafted flea-market items.

If your crafts require special care, be sure to include the instructions with each purchase. For instance, the silverware on *pages 196–199* and the snack trays on *pages 204–207* should be washed by hand only.

gem-topped jars

Ornamental wood shapes turn ordinary jars into containers fit for a king. Painted with acrylic paints, the wood accents are highlighted with a shiny varnish top coat. These vivid vessels hold everything from game pieces to hair bows. Create them using a multitude of colors and wood shapes.

What you need

Clean jar with lid
Newspapers
White spray primer
Wood shapes such as checkers, finials, wooden rings, and small wooden plugs
Acrylic paints in green, black, magenta, yellow, red, turquoise, purple, and orange
Paintbrushes
Clear adhesive, such as Liquid Nails
Spray gloss varnish

What to do

1. Wash and dry the jars. In a well-ventilated area, lay the jar lid on newspapers and spray two light, even coats of white primer, letting it dry between coats.
2. Paint the base color on the lid. Paint each wood shape using the photograph, *opposite*, for ideas. Paint the sections on finials using different colors. Add stripes, dots, or whatever designs you wish. To make dots, dip the handle end of a paintbrush into paint and dot onto surface. To paint the checkers, paint the entire checker black, filling in the grooves. Let dry. Use a small flat brush with a little white paint and brush lightly over the raised surfaces where you want to add color. (By applying white paint before the color, the color will be more vivid.) Let the white paint dry. Repeat the same painting process, using a color over the white. Let the paint dry.
3. Use a small dab of clear adhesive to affix the wood pieces to the lid. Let dry.
4. In a well-ventilated area, lay the jar lids on newspaper and spray with gloss varnish. Let the varnish dry. Apply a second coat if necessary. Let the varnish dry.

Sources

Jars are readily available at the grocery store. Take note of all the interesting shapes and sizes of jars available with metal lids.

Crafting tip

- When painting any bright or light color over black, like on the checkers, it helps to apply a layer of white paint over the black. This will help the color cover better.

Cost to make project

$2 to $3 using recycled jars

Suggested selling price

$7 to $20, depending on size and details on lid

Time to make project

1½ hours

Timesaving tip

- Paint checkers for many jars at once. Paint many lids at once. Assemble wood pieces onto the lids after all pieces are painted, and spray-varnish many of them all lined up on one piece of newspaper.

TO SELL IT

- Display suggested uses for gift-giving on your crafts table. Fill decorated jars with things, such as candy, money, marbles, gift certificates, etc.
- Arrange various sizes and designs together and at different heights to make presentation and selection more interesting. Arrange them to look like sets and even suggest functional uses, like a set for a bathroom filled with cotton balls, bubble bath, wash cloths, or a larger set for the kitchen filled with rice, beans, chocolate chips, etc.

TO GIVE IT

- Fill a decorated jar with wrapped candies to thank a coworker or neighbor for helping you out.
- For someone who enjoys woodworking, fill several coordinating jars with small items such as nails, screws, and washers.

celebration candleholders

For an informal gathering or a grand event, these painted candleholders will help brighten the celebration. Choose wood or glass candleholders, then let this assortment provide the inspiration for the painting and trim.

genie candleholder

rustic pillar
candleholder

"bead-dazzled"
taper holder

daisy
candleholder

color-splashed
candleholder

189

celebration candleholders

genie candleholder
(As shown on page 188)

What you need
Newspapers
Wood candleholder
White spray primer
Metallic acrylic paints in
 copper, red, purple, blue,
 and green
Paintbrush
Gems in desired shapes
Clear adhesive, such as
 Liquid Nails

What to do
1. In a well-ventilated area, cover the work surface with newspapers. Place the candleholder in center of newspapers and spray on a light coat of white primer. Let the paint dry. Spray on a second coat if needed. Let the paint dry.
2. Paint entire piece copper. Using the photograph on *page 188* for ideas, add accents of red, purple, blue, and green. Let the paint dry.
3. Glue the gems onto the candleholder using clear adhesive. Let it dry.

"bead-dazzled" taper holder
(As shown on page 189)

What you need
Newspapers
Wood candleholder
White spray primer
Acrylic paints in yellow, red,
 and blue
Paintbrush
Gloss varnish
Wire cutter
Beading wire
Multicolored beads
Pencil

What to do
1. In a well-ventilated area, cover the work surface with newspapers. Place the candleholder in center of newspapers and spray on a light coat of white primer. Let the paint dry. Spray on a second coat if needed. Let the paint dry.

rustic pillar candleholder
(As shown on page 189)

What you need
Newspapers
Pillar candleholder
Acrylic paints in blue, red,
 cream, and black
Paintbrush
Crackling medium

2. Paint the entire candleholder yellow. Let the paint dry. Using the photograph on *page 189* for ideas, paint on accents of red and blue, following the ridges in the candleholder. Let the paint dry.
3. Paint two or three coats of glossy varnish on the candleholder, letting the varnish dry between coats.
4. Cut a length of beading wire, approximately 12 inches long. Tie a bead on one end and insert the wire through several times. String multicolored beads randomly on the wire until it is filled. At the end of the string of beads, insert the wire through the last bead several times. Tie the string of beads at the bottom of the candleholder, winding upward and looping the strand around twice to secure it. Coil the remaining ends of beads around a pencil and shape to desired coiled shape.

Sandpaper
Wood beads
Clear varnish sealer
12-inch piece of dark red
 suede lacing

What to do
1. Cover your work surface with newspapers. Paint the candleholder black. Let the paint dry.
2. Coat the candleholder (except for bottom) with three coats of crackling medium, allowing to dry between each coat.
3. Following the ridges of the candleholder, paint in cream, red, and blue. Do not brush back and forth over the drying paint, as it will begin to separate and crackle as it dries. Let it dry.
4. Sand the edges of ridges to create a worn look.
5. Paint beads with one thin coat of paint in red and blue. Let the paint dry. Sand the beads to create a worn

effect. Paint the beads with a coat of clear sealer. Let the sealer dry.

6. Tie the dark red suede lace around center of the candleholder. String the beads on ends of the lacing and tie knots on each end to secure the beads.

color-splashed candleholder
(As shown on page 189)

What you need
Glass candleholder
Newspapers
Glass paints in desired colors
Paintbrush

What to do
1. Wash the candleholder and let it dry. Avoid touching the areas to be painted.
2. Starting with one color of paint, make short brushstrokes randomly onto candleholder. Make the strokes from ¼ to 1 inch in length. Continue adding more short strokes using different colors of paint, washing the paintbrush between colors. Let the paint dry.

daisy candleholder
(As shown on page 189)

What you need
Glass candleholder
Newspapers
Glass paints in red, blue, green, yellow, and white
Paintbrush

What to do
1. Wash the candleholder and let it dry. Avoid touching the areas to be painted.
2. Cover the work surface with newspapers. Paint the bottom of the candleholder red. Let the paint dry.
3. Add stripes of color as desired, following the shape of the candleholder. Let dry.
4. To add daisies, use a small round paintbrush to paint five petals for each flower. Let the paint dry. Add a green leaf. Let the paint dry.
5. To make flower centers and other decorative dots, dip the handle end of a paintbrush into paint and carefully dot on the surface. Let the paint dry.

Sources
- Purchase candleholders at flea markets and home decor, discount, and crafts stores.
- Look for crackling medium, usually grouped with the acrylic paints, in crafts and discount stores.

Crafting tips
- If sanding a wood piece to achieve a worn or rustic look, it is a good idea to remove any dust with a tack cloth.
- When crackling, experiment with crackling medium and paint. The more crackle medium and thicker the paint, the bigger the crackle you will achieve. Less crackle medium and thinner paint will result in a finer

crackle. Make sure you use enough crackle medium to get undercoat to show through.

Cost to make project
$1 to $5, depending on the type of candleholder and trims used

Suggested selling price
$4 to $16, depending on time and money invested

Time to make project
½ to 2 hours

Timesaving tip
- To paint several beads at once, fill a thin wood skewer with beads, lay on newspapers, and paint all one color. When dry, roll the beads and finish painting. When the paint is dry, the beads can also be sanded while on the skewer.

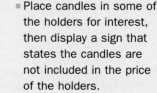

TO SELL IT
- Make sets of candleholders by either selling identical pairs or coordinating mix-and-match pieces.
- Place candles in some of the holders for interest, then display a sign that states the candles are not included in the price of the holders.

TO GIVE IT
- Along with the holders, give a small collection of candles in various colors that coordinate with the holder.

vintage linens
stockings

Vintage linens find their place during the holidays by being turned into lovely Christmas stockings. Dainty lace and satin ribbons drape from each cuff's edge.

193

vintage linens stocking pattern

1 square = 1 inch

What you need
Tracing paper
Pencil
Scissors
18x28-inch vintage or new tea towel for stocking
Vintage or new fabric napkin or tea towel for cuff
Lace
⅛- or ¼-inch-wide ribbon

What to do
1. Enlarge and trace the pattern, *opposite,* and cut out. Use the pattern to cut two front/back stocking shapes from the tea towel. Cut a 1x5-inch piece of fabric for a hanging loop. Cut two corners from napkins or tea towels, each equal to the width of the stocking top and approximately one-half the stocking height.
2. Stitch the stocking pieces with the right sides together using ½-inch seams. Leave the top open. Clip and trim the seam. Turn the stocking to the right side.

3. For the hanging loop, press in ¼ inch along two long edges. Press in half lengthwise and topstitch. Fold the loop in half crosswise and baste the raw edge at the back seam. Seam the cuff in a continuous loop.
4. Stitch lace along the bottom edge of cuff. Weave ribbon through the lace if desired and add a bow.
5. Match the side seams with the right side of the cuff to the wrong side of stocking. Stitch around the top edge. Fold the cuff to the right side.

Sources
- Find vintage tea towels at flea markets, thrift shops, and garage sales. For new tea towels (and vintage reproductions) look in home decor, discount, and kitchen stores.

Crafting tips
- When using vintage linens, check the wear of the piece. If the threads are too worn and fragile, the fabric may rip during sewing.
- To weave thin ribbon through lace, you can first thread it through a needle with a large eye.
- Add more vintage charm by sewing tiny buttons below the cuff area.

Cost to make project
$6 per stocking

Suggested selling price
$18 each

Time to make project
1½ hours

Timesaving tips
- Delete the lace and ribbon for an even simpler, more rustic look.
- Layer fabric before cutting pattern pieces. Be sure to reverse the pattern to cut each stocking back.
- Instead of sewing the stocking hanger, make it from a ribbon scrap.
- When cutting fabric, ribbon, even threads, use a sharp pair of scissors.

TO SELL IT
- Attach a label to tell the history of the tea towels, if possible.
- Arrange stockings so they are handled by customers as little as possible to keep them clean and neat.

TO GIVE IT
- To give at Christmas, fill the stocking with vintage cookie cutters or cloths.
- Suggest displaying the stocking year-round filled with artificial berries, flowers, and other seasonal items.

stunning silver

Using mismatched tableware is always fun— so imagine tossing these creative pieces into the mix! Spectacular as serving pieces or at each place setting, this tableware will make any gathering an event to remember.

What you need
Utensils
Sculpey clay in desired colors and white

Plastic rolling pin
Sharp knife

continued on page 198

Sources
- Purchase Scupley clay in discount, crafts, and art supply stores.
- Look for silverware at thrift shops, garage sales, and flea markets.

Crafting tips
- Keep the work area (and your hands) clean to avoid getting dirt and dust in the clay.
- Try to select utensils that are decorative and in good condition below the handle.
- Don't put the clay so far down on the utensil that it will come into contact with food.
- You can mix colors of Sculpey clay by kneading two colors together.

Cost to make project
$2 to $10, depending on value of utensil purchased

Suggested selling price
$8 to $20, depending on value of silver piece and how elaborate

Time to make project
45 minutes per utensil

Timesaving tip
- Make many utensils at a time in an assembly-line manner. Cover all utensils with white at one time and bake all together. Make many long braided pieces. Make many flower shapes. Roll out larger pieces to cover several pieces of silverware. Bake all of the pieces in the oven at the same time.

TO SELL IT
- Have cards made with care instruction: Do not use in dishwasher or microwave. Handwash in warm sudsy water. Do not soak.

TO GIVE IT
- Tie a matching set of serving utensils together with decorative ribbon. You can also bundle a cake server and knife, a set of four small hors d'oeuvre forks, or a set of large serving utensils, such as a gravy ladle, serving spoons, and serving fork.

stunning silver

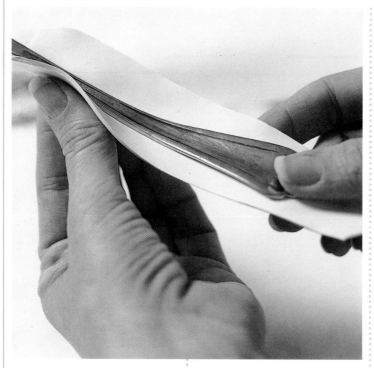

What to do

▲ **1.** Begin with a clean utensil. On a clean flat surface, roll out a ¹⁄₁₆-inch-thick piece of white clay, large enough to cover the utensil handle. The clay should be smooth with an even thickness. Wrap the clay around the handle portion you wish to cover. Cut off the excess clay. Smooth out any wrinkles and blend the clay with fingers so the seam cannot be seen. Bake in the oven according to the directions on the clay label. Allow to cool in oven before removing.

▲ **2.** Once baked and cooled, the white clay on the utensil handle will be hard. Decorate on top of the white clay using various combinations of clay colors. Refer to the photographs on *pages 196–197* for ideas, or make up your own designs. Begin with the largest area to cover first. Roll out a piece of clay in your choice of color. Trim it with a very sharp knife to the size of area you want to cover.

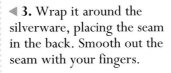

◄ **3.** Wrap it around the silverware, placing the seam in the back. Smooth out the seam with your fingers.

◄▲ **4.** Add small strips of color on the ends or in the middle, wherever you wish. Roll tiny balls of clay between fingers and press onto the clay-covered handle. You can layer different colors of smaller balls on top of larger balls and flatten with fingers onto the colored clay. To make a braided-look trim, roll out two very thin rolls of clay about the width of a toothpick. Lay side by side and twist the two strands together until the clay twists evenly. Place onto the handle and press firmly but gently enough to not flatten the shape. You can coil pieces of clay into a long strip and wind up into a snail shape and add to the handle.

5. When finished decorating, smooth out all clay with fingers. Bake in a preheated oven according to the manufacturer's instructions. Be cautious to not bake too long or too hot. This will cause the colors to turn dark or brownish.

classy case

Bring new life to a tired suitcase by adding a striking floral design. Using a pattern as a guide, this elegant rendition was created with just five colors of acrylic paints.

What you need
Old suitcase
Soapy water and rags
Acrylic paints in black, red, purple, green, and yellow ochre
Small-tipped and medium-size flat paintbrushes
Tracing paper; sharp pencil
Light-colored chalk; tape
Light-colored pencil
Wood skewer, small dowel, or toothpick
Fine-point gold paint pen
Clear sealer

What to do
1. A suitcase of any size will work for this project. Before painting, clean suitcase inside and out with soapy water. Scrub if needed, but do not soak Wipe dry with rag and let air-dry thoroughly.
2. Paint the entire outer surface black or any solid color you like. Let the paint dry.
3. Place tracing paper over the floral and border patterns, *pages 202–203,* and trace with a pencil.

Color the back of the penciled lines with a light colored chalk. Place the tracing paper chalk side down onto painted surface. Tape in place. Draw over the pencil lines with a sharp pencil following all the traced lines. The floral design will transfer onto the black painted surface. If you need to, draw over chalk lines with light-colored pencil. Be careful to not wipe off chalk lines as you work on surface.
4. Paint in solid-colored areas as shown on pattern. To paint the dots, dip the handle end of a paintbrush into paint and dot on the surface. For tiny dots, use a wooden skewer, small dowel, or a toothpick. Let the paint dry. Outline the design with a fine-point gold paint pen. Let it dry.
5. Transfer border pattern, and paint as shown on pattern. Paint the inside of the suitcase with at least two coats of acrylic paint and let dry.
6. Paint a coat of clear acrylic sealer over entire surface. Let it dry and apply a second coat. Let it dry.

Sources
- Find inexpensive suitcases at flea markets and thrift shops. Also, some newer children's suitcases can be found at garage sales.

Crafting tips
- Use quality paintbrushes and maintain them properly.
- If desired, you can cover any metal clasps and hinges or the handle with masking tape before painting. This will help ensure they don't receive any unwanted drips of paint.
- You may need to paint two base coats, depending on the color and condition of the case. If you do, let the paint dry between coats.

Cost to make project
$2 to $10 per suitcase

Suggested selling price
$14 to $28, depending on the size of the suitcase and the intricacy of the design

Time to make project
3½ hours

Timesaving tip
- Purchase only suitcases that are in relatively good shape and that have simple details to paint. Avoid purchasing suitcases that have a lot of details or awkward seams. Make sure clasps work to avoid making repairs

TO SELL IT
- For each size of suitcase, list items that will fit inside.
- Sign the suitcase as a mark of originality. This adds perceived value to the suitcase.

TO GIVE IT
- For grandparents, fill the suitcase with very special photographs of grandchildren, letters, and special creations made by children.
- A painted suitcase can serve as a nice gift basket to hold a variety of different themed items, such as stationery, bath supplies, or sheet music.

floral pattern

paint diagram

border pattern

party snack trays

Used once upon a time
for ladies' luncheons, these
plate-and-cup duos are making a grand
comeback when gilded with the gift of paint.

205

party snack trays

What you'll need

*Glass snack tray and
coordinating cup or other
glassware pieces as desired
Glass paints, such as Liquitex
Glossies High Gloss Acrylic
Enamels, in desired colors
Paintbrushes
Pencil with round-tip eraser,
if desired*

What to do

1. Wash the glass snack set
with dish soap. Rinse well
and let the glassware dry.
Avoid touching any areas
that you intend to paint.
2. Using the photographs,
pages 204–206, for
inspiration, decide how you
would like to paint your
snack set. On the tray, only
the bottom of the tray is to
be painted. On the cup, only
the outside, 1 inch below
the rim, is to be painted. You
can paint the handle. Do not
paint any areas that will
come into contact with food
or drink. If the glassware
piece you have chosen is not
to be used with food, you
can paint both sides of the
piece, if desired.
3. To paint stripes or dots on
the tray, be sure to paint
them *before* applying any
background color. To make
stripes, use a flat brush for
wider stripes and a liner
brush for narrower stripes.
To make dots, simply dip the
handle end of a paintbrush
or a round-tip pencil eraser
into paint and carefully dot
onto the surface. Be sure not
to use too much paint or it
will run or bubble. On the

cup, you may want to dot
one side and let it dry before
adding dots to the other. The
consistency of your paint
will help you determine this.
If you wish to outline any
areas, use a thin liner brush
to paint the outline and let
the paint dry before applying
any background color or
pattern.
4. Depending on the set you
are painting, you may want
to enhance a pattern in the
glass or create a pattern of
your own. To enhance a
design in the glass, decide
what colors you wish to use.
Then simply paint in the
patterns as desired. Be sure
not to rework the paint
while it is wet or it may pull
away from the glassware or
create a rough surface. You
can practice in a small area
first, then simply wash the
paint off before it dries.
Once again, be sure to avoid
touching any areas to be
painted. If creating your own
pattern, remember that the
paint you apply first on the
tray will be the "top" coat
when the piece is turned
over. If painting more than
one coat, be sure to let the
paint dry thoroughly
between coats.
5. To make the paint
permanent, you may need to
bake the glassware after it
has dried. Read the
manufacturer's instructions
on the label. If you do bake
your glassware, let it cool in
the oven before removing.

Sources

- Look for glass snack sets
in thrift shops, flea
markets, garage sales, and
antiques stores.

Crafting tips

- Be sure to follow the
manufacturer's label on
the paint.
- Some paints will be
dishwasher safe if the
painted glass piece is
baked in the oven—read
the paint label.
- Unless mixing paints, use
the paint right from the jar
instead of putting some
amounts on a palette (this
eliminates wasted paint).

- Mix the paints well before
beginning a project.

Cost to make project
$1 for a set

Suggested selling price
$5 for a cup and tray set;
$18 for a set of four; $25 for
a set of six

Time to make project
15 to 45 minutes per set

Timesaving tips

- Paint several of the same
cups, then paint the
matching trays.
- Wash all of the glassware
in the dishwasher before
beginning. Let each piece
dry and cool before
applying paint.

TO SELL IT

- Display only one set from
each glass pattern—have
the others boxed.

- Display a pair of luncheon
sets with decorated cookies
and coordinating napkins.
- Discount the price on a set
of four or six.

TO GIVE IT

- Fill the cup with packaged
teas or coffees before
wrapping the set.
- Give two sets of painted
glassware with a pair of
linen napkins.

- Use a picnic basket to give
a luncheon set to special
friends or family members.
- Tie ribbon bows around
the cup handles before
wrapping the gift.

charming chairs

multicolored chair

Rescued from thrift shops, each of these chairs uses paint to give it a fresh, updated look. Whoever rests on one of these beauties will surely be sitting pretty!

crackled
flower chair

rose chair

charming chairs

crackled flower chair

(As shown on page 209)

What you need

Chair
Sandpaper
Acrylic paints in aqua, coral, yellow ochre, green, and taupe; paintbrush
Crackle medium
Wood shapes, such as flowers and leaves
Wood glue
Brown antiquing gel
Clear sealer
Gold Rub 'n' Buff

What to do

1. Sand off all rough spots from wood surface of chair. (Our chair was unpainted and had a stained and varnished finish.)
2. Paint the chair aqua. Let it dry.
3. Paint at least two heavy coats of crackle medium over the aqua-colored paint. Let dry.
4. Paint a heavy coat of coral paint over the dried crackle medium. Allow it to dry and crackle. Do not brush it while it is drying.
5. Paint two heavy coats of crackle medium over the coral paint. Allow it to dry.
6. Paint a coat of taupe-colored paint over all the layers and allow it to crackle as it dries.

Let it dry very thoroughly before the next step.
7. Paint the leaves and flowers next. Paint leaves green, flower coral with a yellow ochre center. Let dry.
8. Lightly with a dry brush, paint taupe-colored paint over the flower, just highlighting it. Let dry.
9. Glue flower and leaves to chair back.
10. Sand edges and raised areas with sandpaper, just enough to give a worn look.
11. Paint brown antiquing gel over entire surface, painting well into crevices and corners. As it begins to dry, wipe off gently with a soft cloth.
12. Paint clear sealer over entire surface.
13. Highlight raised areas with a very slight amount of gold Rub 'n' Buff. Place a small amount on fingertips and gently rub over raised areas.

multicolored chair

(As shown on page 208)

What you need

An ornate chair
Acrylic paints in black, red, green, purple, blue, yellow, or other colors as you wish
Paintbrush
Clear acrylic varnish

What to do

1. Paint the chair a solid color (we used black), filling in all the crevices.
2. Begin painting sections different colors, allowing the black background to show through in the crevices. Paint the spindles as desired.
3. Let paint dry and apply a clear coat of varnish.

rose chair

(As shown on page 209)

What you need

Chair; sandpaper
Acrylic wood primer
Acrylic paints in deep red, purple, pink, yellow ochre, dark green, dark blue, lime green, and metallic gold
Paintbrushes
Small natural cosmetic sponge
Stiff ½-inch flat paintbrush
Crafts knife
Clear acrylic varnish
Gold Rub 'n' Buff

What to do

1. Prepare surfaces by lightly sanding and priming wood. Choose smooth surfaces to be painted deep red, such as the legs and front and back surfaces of vertical chair back pieces. These will be painted last.
2. When creating multicolored relief sponge painting, reserve darkest

colors for deepest crevices, layering colors from darkest to lightest, and using less paint for each layer. End with lightest color on most-raised surface.

▲ **3.** To paint relief areas on chair, use a sponging technique. Use a palette of deep red, purple, pink, and yellow ochre, on an area, such as the rose, *above.* Use the very deep red for overall base color. Paint the deep crevices using deep red and vibrant purple. Apply these two colors quickly without allowing them to dry. The colors will somewhat blend together.
▼ **4.** Before totally dry, but still tacky, use a clean damp

sponge and very lightly blend the purple and red together just enough to eliminate harsh brush strokes. Do not overwork. Allow the paint to dry.

▲ **5.** To highlight raised areas, use a sponge and thinned pink paint to gently dab on soft highlights. Repeat with a light ochre color. Do not overpaint.

▲ **6.** Paint leaf areas with dark green, using dark blue for deep crevices; blend using a sponge. After dry, apply a light layer of turquoise and a light layer of lime green for the highlights.

7. For remaining surfaces, paint deep blue and sponge with thinned turquoise, using techniques as for relief areas; allow to dry. Next, paint the previously reserved areas deep red. Allow paint to dry thoroughly.

▲ **8.** To splatter-paint surfaces, use a stiff, coarse ½-inch flat paintbrush and deep red and metallic gold paints. Dip brush into one paint at a time. Use a crafts knife to scrape across the bristles.

9. Seal the chair with varnish. Using finger, very lightly apply a small amount of gold Rub 'n' Buff to the most raised areas. Rub off with a soft rag. Seal the chair a second time.

Sources
- Purchase chairs at a reasonable price from thrift shops, garage sales, flea markets, and auctions.
- Look for crackle medium in paint, art, crafts and discount stores.

Crafting tip
- Use plenty of crackle medium. It may take three or even four coats. Don't overbrush the paint as it begins to dry.

Cost to make project
$10 to $20 per chair

Suggested selling price
$40 to $75 per chair

Time to make project
3 to 6 hours

Timesaving tip
- Choose chairs with less intricate designs to minimize decorative painted details.

TO SELL IT
- Be willing to hold purchased chairs for customers while they shop.
- If you can purchase matching chairs, paint two or four using the same colors and design. Then sell the chairs in sets.

TO GIVE IT
- Give these one-of-a-kind chairs as a memory-making housewarming gift.
- For special youngsters, purchase chairs, rockers, or tables made for children. Personalize each piece by using a child's favorite colors, motifs, and sayings on the piece of furniture.

JAR TAGS

Strawberry Jam

These tags will add pizzazz to kitchen creations, such as jellies and jams. The elastic cord slips around any size jar. The center of the tag is a premade label, making it an easy-to-write-on surface. These pretty labels keep things organized and also make great gift tags.

What you need
Heavyweight paper or tagboard
Straight or decorative-edge scissors
Brush pens in desired colors
Metallic gold permanent marker
1½x2¾-inch white adhesive labels
⅛-inch paper punch
Gold elastic cording

What to do
1. Cut the tagboard or heavy paper into a 3½x1½-inch strip using a straight or decorative-edged scissors. If desired, cut the corners off the paper strip.

2. Color the paper piece using a brush pen. Carefully outline the edges of the paper piece using a gold marker. Outline the adhesive label with gold. Center the label on the cut piece of paper and press into place.
3. Punch a small hole into each end. Cut a 6-inch length of gold elastic cording. Thread the cording through the holes; knot the ends to secure. Leave the label blank for the customer to fill in.

Sources
- Purchase brush pens in crafts and art stores.
- Purchase gold elastic cording in crafts and discount stores.
- Purchase adhesive labels in discount and office supply stores.

Crafting tip
- Knot the elastic cording on the front side of the tags so they can be easily slipped over jars and bottles.

Cost to make project
10¢ each

Suggested selling price
6 for $2, 12 for $3.50

Time to make project
5 minutes per tag

Timesaving tips
- Layer and cut two or three pieces of paper at once.
- Purchase gold-edged labels to eliminate the outlining in step 2.
- Layer three or four cutout tags and punch the holes through several tags at a time.
- Use colored papers for the background instead of coloring white paper with a brush pen.
- Select a pretty, easy-to-read font, and print the labels on a computer.

TO SELL IT
- Display various ways of using the tags.
- Sell the tags in sets. Make half of the sets the same design; mix up the remaining half.

TO GIVE IT
- Attach these labels to homemade jellies, sauces, pickles, and more.
- Place a dozen labels in a canning jar to give to someone who likes to do canning.

INDEX

CREDITS & TIPS

Designers

Susan M. Banker—10, 24, 28–30, 36, 52, 132–133, 142, 144–146, 154, 164–167, 172, 180, 189, and 204–206.

Sharon Barrett—92.

Tess Bournke—88.

Donna Chesnut—100–101, 104, 106, 108–109, 114, 116–117, 122, and 178.

Gaylen Chesnut—100–101, 104, 106, 108–109, 114, 116–117, 122, and 178.

Carol Dahlstrom—116–117 and 122.

Phyllis Dobbs—128 and 138.

Phyllis Dunstan—84 and 212.

Barbara Sestok—20–21, 38, and 70–72.

Margaret Sindelar—44, 46–47, 48, 56–57, 58–59, 64–69, 76, 78, and 192–193.

Alice Wetzel—14, 18, 32, 150, 152, 160, 170, 174, 186, 188–189, 196, 200, and 208–209.

Photographers

Andy Lyons Cameraworks, Peter Krumhardt, Scott Little

Photostyling

Carol Dahlstrom

Photostyling Assistant

Donna Chesnut

Show-Time Tips

Selling your crafts at shows, bazaars, or other venues is one way to share your talents and turn an enjoyable hobby into a business. These tips will get you started and help you have a fun and profitable crafts show.

Start small by signing up for a local crafts show. After displaying your works of art locally once or twice, you'll know if you want to turn your passion into a business.

To find out where and when crafts shows are in your area, consult the Chamber of Commerce, local art and crafts guilds, churches, and newspapers. Churches often have crafts bazaars with a minimal charge per space, while larger shows may charge a higher fee. You will have to decide how much money you want to invest at a show before applying. Along with the space fee, consider costs for display props, transporting, and packaging your crafts.

In preparation for a show, work throughout the year on the crafts you will display. Waiting until the last minute will cause tension and take the fun out of the experience.

As you work, price the completed items and carefully pack them away, using white tissue paper to avoid any damage. Set a goal for what you want to have ready for a show and record what you have on hand.

If you don't have a tax ID number, you may need to acquire a temporary one. Consult your local tax office.

At least one week before the show, make a list of everything you will need. Along with your handcrafted items be sure to bring a cash box and change, the inventory list, business cards, bags, tape, a calculator, wrapping materials, pens and pencils, receipt slips, scissors, and display props. You may also need chairs, extension cords, a sewing kit, or glues. As you pack for the show, check off each item so nothing is forgotten.

After you set up, check out the other crafts. Throughout the day, watch what's selling. As your sales ring up, mark off each item on the inventory list. At the end of the show, tally your sales. Hopefully you'll find that you had a successful show. With time and experience, you can turn your hobby into a fun business. Don't forget, the wonderful crafts you get to take home after the show is over make great gifts!

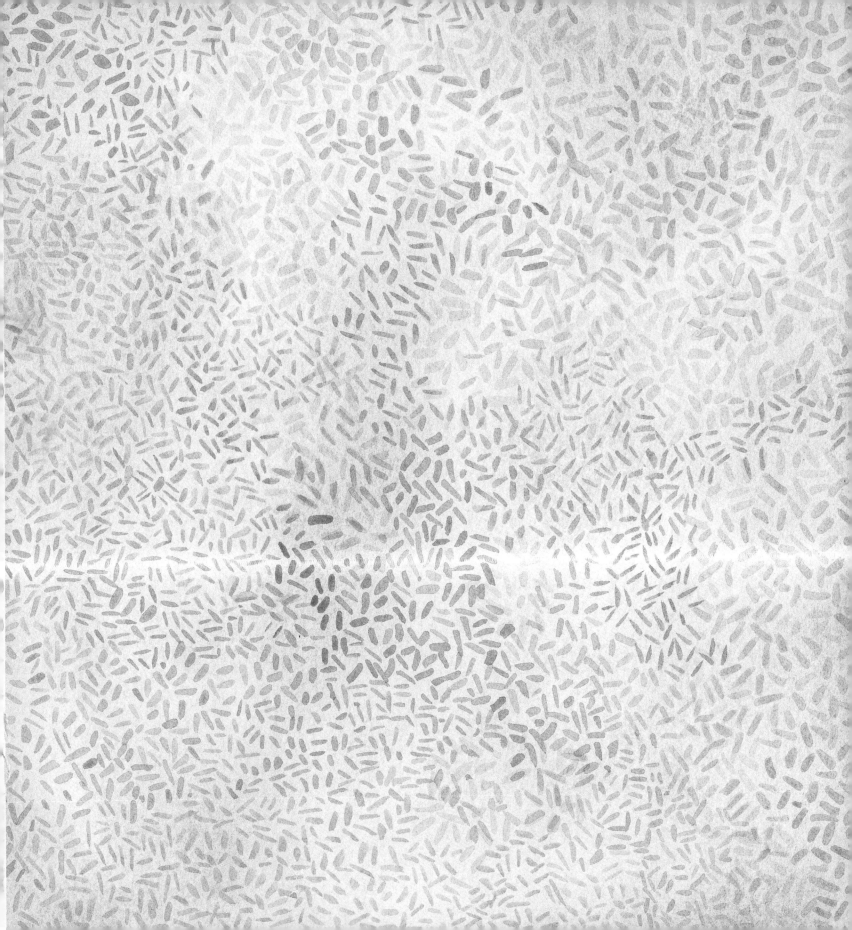

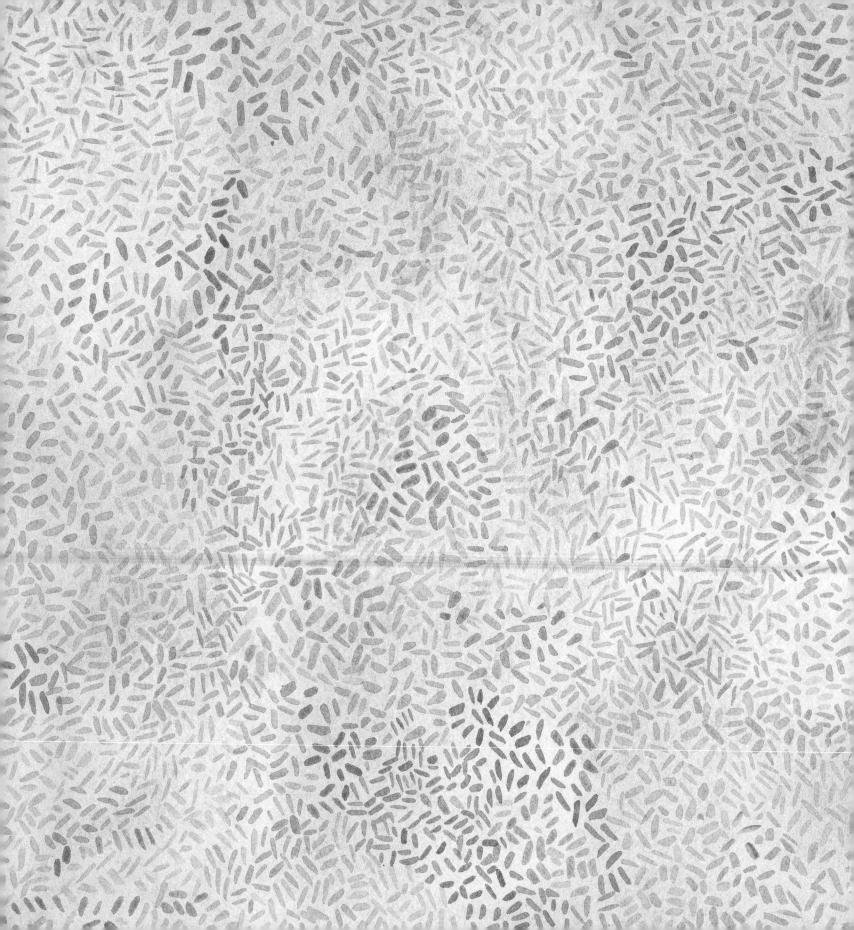